The Point of View
for my work as an author

SØREN KIERKEGAARD AS A YOUTH

A pencil sketch, made by a cousin, CHRISTOPHER KIERKEGAARD, *for S.K.'s favourite cousin,* JULIE KIERKEGAARD

Søren Kierkegaard

THE POINT OF VIEW
FOR MY WORK
AS AN AUTHOR

A REPORT TO HISTORY
and related writings

TRANSLATED WITH INTRODUCTION AND NOTES BY
WALTER LOWRIE · NEWLY EDITED WITH A PREFACE
BY BENJAMIN NELSON

HARPER TORCHBOOKS ❦ THE CLOISTER LIBRARY
HARPER & BROTHERS, NEW YORK

CONTENTS

CONTENTS

Editor's Notice and Acknowledgment

Two directly autobiographical 'communications' by Søren Kierkegaard, each followed by its own supplement, are included in the following pages. The more important and comprehensive statement, *The Point of View for my Work as an Author*, was written in 1848 but waited for another decade before it was posthumously published by the author's brother in 1859. The closing Postscript to the significant supplement, 'The Individual', is dated March 1855 and carries us to the hour of Kierkegaard's ultimate attack upon the Established Church of Denmark. He died eight months later, on 11 November 1855.

The shorter 'accounting' here offered as *My Activity as a Writer* was issued along with its supplement in 1851 as a token of what was yet to come.

Two contributions by Mr. Lee M. Capel to the present edition deserve special acknowledgment here. The new text of 'The Individual' incorporates many—technical limitations forbade use of all—of his proposed emendations to the rendering by Dr. Walter Lowrie. Also, Mr. Capel has furnished readings of several hitherto untranslated fragments from Kierkegaard's *Journal* directly bearing on the latter's interpretations of his authorship. Two of these are made available in a closing section of the present work.

B. N.

PREFACE TO THE TORCHBOOK EDITION

by

Benjamin Nelson

ONE shattering paragraph crowds hard upon the next in the overwhelming 'Report to History' by the eccentric Danish genius of whom we are to speak in this Preface. Consider the following four entries, each inscribed in a slightly different mood, from the professedly 'certified' audit of his literary and personal existence—what he insisted on calling his 'work as an author':

> If Copenhagen ever has been of one opinion about anybody, I venture to say that it was of one opinion about me, that I was an idler, a dawdler, a *flâneur*, a frivolous bird, intelligent, perhaps brilliant, witty, &c.—but as for 'seriousness', I lacked it utterly. I represented a worldly irony, *joie de vivre*, the subtlest form of pleasure-seeking—without a trace of 'seriousness and positivity'; on the other hand, I was prodigiously witty and interesting.[1] . . .

However, in this accounting I must make a more precise reckoning of the share Governance had in the authorship. For in case I were to affirm out and out that from the very first instant I had a survey of the whole authorship, or that at every moment, stage by stage, I had by anticipation so far exhausted the possibilities that later reflection had not taught me anything, nor even this other thing, that though what I had done was surely right, yet only afterwards was I in a position to understand thoroughly that this was so—if I were to do this, it would be a denial of God and dishonesty towards Him. No, I must say truly that I cannot understand the whole, just because to the merest insignificant detail I understand the whole, but what I cannot understand is that now I can understand it and yet cannot by any means say that at the instant of commencing it I understood it so precisely—though it is I that have carried it out and made every step with reflection. In the parlance of pure bosh one could easily explain this by saying, as someone has said of me, without having any conception of my literary work as a totality, that I had a genius for reflection.[2] . . .

And now as for me, the author, what, according to my opinion, is my relation to the age? Am I perhaps the 'Apostle'? Abominable! I have never given an occasion for such a judgement. I am a poor insignificant person. Am I then the teacher, the educator? No, not at all; I am he who himself has been educated, or whose authorship expresses what it is to be educated to the point of becoming a Christian. In the fact that education is pressed upon me, and in the measure that it is pressed, I press in turn upon this age; but I am not a teacher, only a fellow student.[3] ...

The expression I use is, that in relation to the intellectual and religious fields, and with a view to the concept of existence, and hence to the concept of Christianity, I am like a spy in a higher service, the service of the idea. I have nothing new to proclaim; I am without authority, being myself hidden in a deceit; I do not go to work straightforwardly but with indirect cunning; I am not a holy man; in short, I am a spy who in his spying, in learning to know all about questionable conduct and illusions and suspicious characters, all the while he is making inspection is himself under the closest inspection. Observe that this is the sort of people the police make use of.[4] ...

Dare we lend credence to so provocative and paradoxical a writer?

What purposes did he expect to be served by a document conceived in this spirit?

Does the author's 'point of view' have anything to say to us, more than a century removed from his mystifying life and even more mystifying death?

I

Established maxims of law and logic warn us against taking anyone's testimony concerning himself at face value. Equally familiar canons of literary criticism charge us to decide an author's artistic intention on the basis of his completed achievement rather than his inchoate personal history or his programmatic recollections. And who today needs to be cautioned about the power of unconscious fantasy, the omnipresence of projection, and the masks without number of the 'mechanisms of defense'?

On these scores and on so many others, Kierkegaard proves to be a mighty exception. When his turn came to present a chart of his soul's itinerary, he struggled to do so with such searing integrity as to make all these prudent reminders seem trivial and pedantic.

Whatever the rules of procedure dictate, the hearing of his case can hardly begin unless we accept him, initially at least, as his own advocate and witness, and his 'Report to History' as more than a merely plausible deposition by a heavily-interested party. Indeed, to obey scholarly stipulations against 'genetic fallacies' literally would be to forfeit the chance of having as our guide the only man qualified to initiate a solution of the mystifying puzzles of his life and art. A prime aesthetic consideration, to speak of no other for the moment—the sheer need to understand the intricate structure of his authorship—would seem to dictate that we adopt his hypothesis that his lifelong efforts acquired their deepest meanings when they were construed as artful designs arranged to compel his countrymen to acknowledge and to abandon the amnesia of their spirits. As for psychoanalysis, Kierkegaard made his own historic journey within, exploring depths no less remote than those which were to be encountered by Freud. Nor did he have to wait for Freud to devise a repertoire of psychological strategies, as yet, unsurpassed in their distinctive sphere, for bestirring those who lived lives of noisy desperation in adamant resistance against their spiritual callings.

His biographers have presented him in a hundred guises, depending on *their* 'points of view'.[5] He has been portrayed as a would-be Don Juan, a crippled Oedipus, 'an endogenous manic-depressive with an atypical career', an 'emaciated schizophrenic', an enemy of the liberal spirit of '48, a monarchist ideologue, a reactionary obscurantist—even a vulgar anti-semite. His admirers have hailed him as a peerless diarist, the liberator of philosophy from the deadly embrace of Hegelian panlogism, the founder of the existentialist view of life, the herald of crisis theology, the nineteenth century's truest witness to the Passion.

Evidence can be found to sustain many variant versions of his life but we shall never move with any assurance in the universe Kierkegaard so cunningly contrived unless we have attempted the experiment of regarding his *Point of View* as the decisive (not the only!) word on his life and authorship. Admittedly, *The Point of View* we may encounter at the close of our researches will seem much more complicated than *The Point of View* we confronted at the outset. A worse fate awaits us, however, if we seek to know Kierkegaard without availing ourselves of his own obviously biased 'Report to History'. We condemn ourselves to a long drawn-out period of clutching at shadows. The Kierkegaards we shall devise in the interim will be creatures of our fantasy; we need *The Point of View* to help arrange the cues leading to his innermost *sanctum*.

The piercing lyricism and the flashing dialectic of his paradoxical inventions in the aesthetic and ethical mode—such as his *Either/Or* (1843), *Stages on Life's Way* (1845)—may tempt the unwary reader today as they tempted his contemporaries in the 1840's to identify this melancholy 'knight of faith' as a Danish Faust who was never so attractive and so successful as when he was vigorously crossing swords with the witty and worldly disciples of Goethe and Hegel. Many will suppose, as his fellow-citizens of Copenhagen supposed, that the alternation of these pseudonymous masterpieces with devout, sometimes even simpering 'Edifying Discourses' over his own name only meant that, for reasons best known to himself, one who was called to be a Titan still hankered to be a country parson.

The Point of View leaves one no option but to reconsider his 'work as an author'—his personal existence as well as his art—from the commanding perspective of his spiritual calling. In his own eyes, he warned from the outset, he was none of the characters he affected to play in his masterworks of imagination; neither the rakish adventurer, nor the virtuoso of the arts, nor the sober citizen, nor the scientific psychologist, nor the political partisan, nor the philosophical polemicist, nor the scriptural exegete, nor the theological martinet, nor the religious enthusiast.

His *Point of View* contends that even when his delighted readers supposed he was engaged in captivating their senses and flattering their vanities, he was already fishing for their souls as part of his unique mission *in partibus FIDELIUM*, using bait especially prepared to lure worldly-wise outward Christians. Early in the course of his authorship, he insists, he had become convinced that entirely new resources would need to be deployed if his contemporaries were to be converted from the nominal religion hardly different from paganism, which they professed—namely *Christendom*—to the *Christianity* proclaimed by Christ and Luther. He saw clearly that none of the inherited *direct* methods of quickening spirits—not friendly counsel, neighborly admonitions, learned explanations, moral censure, canonical penalties, not even the personal suffering of a martyr ('immediate pathos')—sufficed any longer to dislodge his contemporaries from their havens of self-satisfaction and indifference.

This awareness of the total irrelevance, even harmfulness, of the traditional apologetics, had led him to experiment with hitherto unknown strategies of psychological warfare and to project a new *para-military science* suitable for his 'age of dissolution'[6] when the 'individual' happily lost himself in collectives of every description: the prevailing intellectual 'System' and mode of 'Speculation'; the claims of history; the demands of 'public opinion' and the 'human race'; the entire establishment, religious as well as civil.

His deeds and works became a series of contrived camouflages and 'deceptions', illustrating the adventures of his pseudonymous heroes and heroines (his *alter egos*) among the blandishments in every sphere of human existence as they passed through what Kierkegaard called the 'stages on life's way'.[7] Through such 'experiments' in *indirect* communication, he insinuated the despair and futility which attended every one of man's evasions of authentic response to the Unconditional: the lures of the purely aesthetic orientation to experience, the idolatries of science, the seductions of ethics, the shams of legalism and the make-believe of conventional religion.[8]

These roles, he now proclaims in his *Point of View*, were only masks which he assumed in the interest of faithfully discharging his responsibilities to his Divine Governance by whom, he was convinced, he had been co-opted, more for his follies than for his powers, to conduct a critical mission in the capacity of a *spy in the higher service of an idea*. His task was to provide a public example of what was involved in *becoming a Christian* at a time when everyone blandly supposed himself to *be one* by accident of birth.

The author's guide and teacher through all these byways was the wondrous Socrates[9] who had devoted his life to setting an example and embodying a paradigm, compelling his indifferent contemporaries by his odd acts and odder questions to know themselves so that they might pursue the good in deepest inwardness. Following in the footsteps of Socrates, he entered upon the two forks of the road which must be traversed by everyone who wishes to experience the fullness of his being and time; the unaccompanied journey into the interior of self and the exposed life of the 'double agent' who daily ventures abroad into the streets to share the common out-of-doors activities of his unsuspecting neighbors. Emulating Socrates, he braved the perils of the exhausting quest for 'the individual' with no other shields than his cherished gifts of irony and faith. To appreciate how badly Kierkegaard was buffeted both by his own inner demons and his insensitive contemporaries, we need to supplement what he tells us in the *Point of View* by such works as *Sickness Unto Death* (1849), *The Concept of Dread* (1844), *The Present Age* (1846), and above all, his *Journal*. Nonetheless, he persevered through every adversity and attack and became his century's greatest craftsman in the arts of uncovering and portraying the snares and triumphs of man's existence. His fantastic experiments as author and actor more than vindicated his claim to be the 'Master of Irony', a title he claimed in the manner of a medieval scholar to commemorate the fact that he had completed his academic apprenticeship with the study of the wiles of Socrates as portrayed in the works of Plato, Xenophon, and Aristophanes.

We need not wonder, therefore, that few philosophers since Aristotle have given us such deep insights into the funadmentals of poetics and rhetoric as has Kierkegaard. From his M.A. thesis on the (Socratic) *Concept of Irony* (1841) to his sounding of the alarms in *The Instant* (1855), translated into English under the title, *The Attack upon Christendom*, Kierkegaard engaged in continuous experimentation with vehicles and modes of expression: *direct* communication, *indirect* communication, existential reflection, dialectical lyric, *diapsalmata*, edifying discourse, Christian sermon, and so on.[10]

Yet we would misjudge his intention if we supposed that it was the hope of winning immortality as a virtuoso in the realms of art which decided him to engage in these experiments. Had this been the whole story, there would be no explaining why he strained so hard to learn what he called the 'secret art of helping others' in the face of their stubborn refusal to help themselves. History has known few men who have been so intent upon mastering the uncanny skills of irritating their fellows into risking the achievement of authentic selfhood so that they might respond with their whole being to the claims of the Unconditioned. In the eyes of Freud, indeed, Kierkegaard's insistence on 'deceiving the deceivers' into facing up to the truth would doubtless have seemed a disturbing case of *furor therapeuticus*, a pathological obsession with healing someone, likely to interfere with the conduct of a neutral scientific *analysis* of the psyche of the patient.

Kierkegaard could (and would!) have responded to Freud that the established resources of classical analysis hardly sufficed to effect recovery in the difficult cases which confronted the true shepherd of *souls*. In contemporary parlance, Kierkegaard might be said to have been primarily concerned with the treatment of those suffering from crippling disturbances in their sense of identity owing to narcissistic impairments and cultural incoherence. His repertoire of the tactics for the personal appropriation of and the induction of others into the meaning of existence is rich beyond description. Whatever be their persuasion, contemporary psychotherapists would do well to ponder his teachings on the meanings and uses of irony, ambiguity, incognito, the 'maieutic' attitude, conscious duplicity, 'existential reduplication', 'immediate pathos', 'causing to take notice', 'accepting the other's illusions (and pretensions) as real money', 'teleological suspensions of the ethical', 'repetition' as contrasted with 'recollection'.[11] To appreciate to what extent Kierkegard pioneered in these areas, we need to keep the master 'clinicians' and strategists—Aristotle, Machiavelli, Pascal, Freud, and many others—at our elbow at all times.

The Point of View carries us to the edge of the last phase of Kierkegaard's journey. As hard as he had labored to excel his mentor, Socrates, in stirring souls to self-examination, he had never ceased to pray that one day, when his own education in 'becoming a Christian' neared its end, he would no longer be burdened by the compulsion to practice mordant reflection and double agency. Then he could come forth from behind his masks with the simplicity of one who had been made whole.

So turbulent a spirit as Kierkegaard's was not to win the peace he prized without an exhausting civil war against his inner demons. To think of himself as an 'Extraordinary One' in the religious sense was at once his temptation and his dread; nor was he free from fear that, for all his pains, he might come to be widely viewed as a merely 'interesting' curiosity or a self-serving eccentric.

In the end, however, he forged for himself the fate he craved. Instead of succumbing to destructive afflictions and excesses as did a number of others, notably Dostoyevsky and Nietzsche, in whose company he is too unreservedly placed these days, he let no day go by without struggling to hold himself in readiness to be 'a witness'. He rededicated himself and his gifts continually to the Life which was for him the Light, the Truth, and the Way. His earthly Waterloo—the Napoleonic assault upon the entire Establishment and its noted paragons in *The Attack upon Christendom*—was his crowning choice. Thus he had fulfilled the often promised act of 'pathos' which stern strategic considerations had repeatedly required him to delay. His reward was a martyr's grave where he had hoped his life would end *and begin*. He was now entered upon the career he had coveted most, becoming an 'absent one'[12] who was everywhere and always present.

II

There is no sign of abatement in the century-old war which has been waging throughout the scholarly world over the meaning of Kierkegaard's entire authorship. The fullest recounting of the struggle established beyond doubt that *The Point of View* locates at the very center of the ground on which the battle rages. With Kierkegaard's *direct* communication as their prime target, the rival camps contend over whether the explanation of the authorship given there is a profound revelation or a perverse distortion of Kierkegaard's life and work.[13]

Despite all this activity, a truly comprehensive analysis of *The Point of View* is not yet available to students. Indeed, we do not yet possess an adequate collation of the extensive remains which throw direct light on the numberless waverings of Kierkegaard's spirit concerning the adequacy of *The Point of View* in defining his image of himself and his mission. The more closely one analyzes the full text of his *Journals*, the more evident it becomes that the secret afterlife of *The Point of View* in the mind of its tormented author cries out for a chronicler endowed with special powers to record and interpret the agonizing vibrations of his questing, twice-born spirit.[14]

The undersigned must be content, at this time, to stress one humble fact: in the midst of the very struggle as to how faithfully or how falsely *The Point of View* describes Kierkegaard's authorship prior to 1848, this 'Report to History' has rarely received the attention it deserves in its own right. The hesitations of Kierkegaard's devoted American biographer and translator may help to illustrate this situation. As much as Dr. Lowrie loved Kierkegaard, his Introduction in the pages immediately following this Preface indicate his embarrassment over how to characterize *The Point of View*. Although profoundly autobiographical, Dr. Lowrie explains, *The Point of View* falls far short of being a biography and may not be compared as a confession or apology with the masterworks in that sphere by Xenophon, St. Augustine or Cardinal Newman. The scintillating tonal contrasts and the 'profound psychological concepts' of the pseudonymous masterpieces are lacking in this 'Direct Communication', he continues, which appears 'solely intent upon emphasizing religious categories' and, therefore, is very far from being an explanation of the Works as a whole.

The present writer finds himself unable to share Dr. Lowrie's reservations. Even if *The Point of View* did not rank (as in our opinion it does) with the mightiest achievements of Kierkegaard's pen, it is destined to achieve an even greater place in the mind and heart of everyone who hopes to know him in the depths. Surely no synoptic 'explanation' of his writings, it offers what no topical concordance could ever provide: *it is an authentic map of his labyrinthine world from his own hand and even if not true down to the last detail, it is an indispensable interpretation of the anguished pilgrimage of an extraordinary spirit.* A powerful conversion experience, culminating in Easter of 1848 doubtless left its mark upon the accounting prepared in the same year, but we dare not jump to the conclusion that *The Point of View* totally falsifies the developments of his earlier years. Kierkegaard's 'Report to History' is, indeed, a backward glance, but it is the backward glance of one who has struggled, as few men ever have, to live the meaning of his life toward the future. Precisely because—as he admitted to himself in his *Journals*—it goes to extremes at points, it permits us to see into one of his secret selves when its innermost core was burning at maximum intensity.

Yet there will surely be a goodly number who will miss—even be strongly tempted to avoid—the full impact of Kierkegaard's design. However, he who has the courage or curiosity to attend to *The Point of View* for an hour may be assured of one thing above all else: the man he meets in these pages shall haunt him for the rest of his days. We may come to think of him as we will—we may find him imprudent, uncivil, frantic, perverse, mad, fanatic, absurd; we may deem him a philosopher without a doctrine, a theologian without faith, a not so extraordinary man consumed by a religious 'will to power', a martyr *to himself* lacking reverence for Being; an unregenerate romantic who could not abandon the pleasures of the 'unhappy conscience';[15] we may even say that he was a 'pathological somnambulist who heralds our dreadful Age of Unreason'—but we will not be able to forget him. Of how many authors and works in the annals of autobiography can this be said?

He was certain that future ages would read his 'Report to History' with intense interest because he knew that he was one of the small number who had a mighty message to communicate to history which history could ill afford to neglect. *The Point of View* is a decisive stage in the evolution of his endeavors to effect this communication.

We dare not skip anything, however. Like every true artist—and dedicated secret agent—Kierkegaard did nothing in vain. His every word is a clue. Each term in the title and sub-titles expresses his ultimate sense of existence and authorship. *The Point of View*, he is telling us, is aimed squarely from his center and is, therefore:

1. a *direct* rather than an indirect *communication* or a dialectical lyric or an edifying discourse or a Christian sermon, and

2. a *report to History* in the sense of an accounting, as contrasted with what he was elsewhere to call a 'psychological experiment', a 'philosophical fragment', a 'confession'.

The telling legend from *Henry IV, Part II* establishes a final emphasis: the reader is given notice that the author intends to judge himself and hopes to be judged by others in the light of his perplexing *purposes* as well as his all too evident *follies*.

On careful reading, *The Point of View* proves to have no fewer than ten purposes: (of how many autobiographies can *this* be said?).

The Point of View is:

1. *First and foremost*, a startling document in a complicated legal proceeding, in fact *a brief in a super-terrestrial trial* whose venue is a site not yet seen by mortal eyes and whose presiding Magistrate is One described by Kierkegaard, the advocate, as his Divine Governance. To say precisely who are the interested parties, and what are the grounds of action is no easy matter since the author of the brief presumes to describe himself as a ward

of the court and alternately acts as prosecutor and defendant. Although Magister K. and Mankind appear to take turns in the witness box and at the advocate's bar, both are, in fact, being weighed in the balances, for this is a dispute over redemption, where the appeal to mercy follows fast upon the appeal to justice.[16] For, as The Poet says, 'in the course of Justice none of us should see salvation'.[17]

Only if we respond vividly to Kierkegaard's ultimate ways of imagining this litigation can we hope to understand the form and matter of *The Point of View* and the hitherto untranslated notes on the brief which are to be found in the *Journal*. This emphasis helps us understand why in the midst of the book its author turns aside from his report and indictment to defend himself from cross-accusations, notably the accusation of misanthropic treachery against mankind.

2. *A bio-bibliographical 'accounting'* of Kierkegaard's literary and intellectual activities from the standpoint of his mission. Great pains are taken here to prove that from the beginning of his authorship, at least since *Either/Or* (1843), the mystifying alternation of his publications—the pseudonymous aesthetic and ethical and openly religious writings—were tactical maneuvers in the interest and under the direction of his Governance.

3. *A pathographical addendum*, offering selected comments concerning the author's story of his misfortunes, failings and follies. Here Kierkegaard speaks poignantly of his boyhood and youth, his father, his fiancée, his Copenhagen cronies, the episode of the *Corsair*, and so on. Far from making pretense to completeness, Kierkegaard plainly acknowledges that he knew more than he wished to say.

4. *A Report to History* recording the author's relations to his 'age of dissolution' and the nature of the mission assigned to him by his Governance. The central theme under this head is his account of his 'experimental education' in *becoming* a Christian.

5. *A Report to his Governance* detailing the conduct of the latter's charge. This report is avowedly written at the instance (but not for the information of) his Governance who already knows the facts of the case infinitely better than does the author of the report. Thus, his Governance will hardly need to be told that even when the author seemed to be deviously playing the role of a double agent, demonically tempting his contemporaries to plunge still further into the pleasures of heedlessness, he was in truth 'a spy in a higher service'—the service of the Governance.

6. *An Accusation directed to his Governance*, describing the ways of men and condition of the world, including a concise *exposé* of the emotional crudities, the moral vanities, the intellectual conceits and spiritual follies of his contemporaries. In this context, the critique of the cultural fashions of his time, characteristically entrusted to a footnote (pages 88–89), is a masterly evocation of a lifetime of thought about philosophy and existence. Here as

elsewhere, particularly in his supplementary Notes about 'The Individual', Kierkegaard lashes out against the exaggerations he most abhors. He inveighs against 'pantheism', the pet illusion—both 'acoustic and optical'—of the witty intelligentsia and the learned clerks of his time; he scores the 'System' and 'Speculation', as he called the essentially pantheistic implications derived by his contemporaries, from Hegel and some of the younger Hegelians of the Left, chiefly Feuerbach. A favorite leitmotif of the 'three magnitudes'—temporal existence, eternity and the Self as an Agent of choice—is subtly orchestrated with explorations of the atonal confusion connected with such notions (we often call them 'clang words' today) as 'society', 'the human race', 'the crowd', 'mankind', 'humanity', 'human species', 'individual specimen', 'the public'.

7. *A public attestation*, an acknowledgment for all to read, of the aliases, pseudonyms, roles, ruses, and 'teleological suspensions of the ethical' resorted to in the authorship and life of one who had from the first gladly accepted the summons to enter the service of a higher power. In this connexion, the author explains, his conscious duplicities were intended to effect a change of heart in his contemporaries—an effort to compel them to confront the Unconditional in deepest inwardness.

8. *A manual* of technical rules and tactical plans for the benefit of those who might have occasion in the future to deceive the self-deceivers into the truth. These rules spell out the strategies to be employed in a campaign of total psychological warfare against all who profane their spiritual callings by indifference, half-heartedness, blind evasions and arrant disobedience.

The penultimate purpose is best indicated by words he himself used in his *Journal* in connexion with the fragment published in 1851 and issued below under the title *My Activity as a Writer*. The pronouncement concerning his 'point of view' he explains, was:

9. *An 'act of transition to another sphere'* aimed to 'turn the tide' in the ongoing battle with his age; a deed intended to forestall the conversion of his authorship into 'a new doctrine'.[18]

And lastly:

10. *The Point of View* is a *premonitory disclosure* of the impending climax of his mission. Such is the intent of his thinly veiled warning that he would before long goad his contemporaries into making him a martyr.[19] Nor should we fail to notice that the Epilogue and Conclusion to the work are reserved for words to be used on his Epitaph and in the course of the eulogy to be spoken at his grave. The final postscript to 'The Individual' precedes his death by only eight months.

As we have intimated above, a biographer of consummate powers will be needed to chronicle the stormy afterlife of *The Point of View* in the mind of its author. Ceaselessly probing his own motives, the intimations of his

Governance, and the needs of his age, he subjected his unpublished 'Report' to microscopic scrutiny, filing one *caveat* after another. One day he took himself to task for having falsely implied that he was a martyr secure in his faith when indeed he was, in a way that even he himself could not truly understand or explain, a poet who was also a penitent. Another day found him impatiently arming himself to begin the decisive battle against the deceivers as the sworn champion of his Governance.[20]

Apparently there were many who thought (or hoped?) that the appearance of *My Activity as a Writer* (in 1851) meant that the author considered his authorship essentially finished. His sophisticated critics did not have to wait long to learn that Kierkegaard could not be counted on to remain silent. He fired salvo after salvo until the very moment death claimed him in the midst of his terrifying attack upon Christendom.[21]

Nor did even death end his authorship. The appearance of *The Point of View* in 1859 initiated a new and exasperating sense of puzzlement which, as we have stressed above, still shows no sign of subsiding. Students of his life and thought are more at odds today than they have ever been over the inner springs of his authorship, nor is any consensus in sight as to how the reckoning in *The Point of View* squares with other evidence we hear about his life and work both before and after 1848.[22]

A younger American scholar has observed that the incorrigibly dialectical Kierkegaard would doubtless have reaped immense pleasure from the persistence of this air of mystery. Perhaps. Perhaps also, mystery—*in every sense of that term*—was Kierkegaard's native element. One who finds this statement and its cryptic emphasis vexing will not have long to wait for redress. Soon enough, luckily, he will be savoring Kierkegaard's *Point of View.*

III

A quick way to approach an answer to our third question would be to survey the existentialist strands in terms of twentieth century life and thought. One may put the matter bluntly: Heidegger, Jaspers, Sartre, Barth, Franz Kafka, and many others are hard to conceive without Kierkegaard. In these terms, his influence is impossible to exaggerate.

Yet there are other senses in which he is still unknown to us. The extraordinary subtlety of his dialectic has been coarsened again and again; the temptation to exploit him for alien purposes has rarely been resisted and no successor has sought, with his purity, to 'will one thing'. It may even be argued that we are far too unfamiliar with the wider sources, contexts and implications of his teachings to interpret his message with true assurance. Certain promising steps have been taken, notably by Karl Loewith,[23] in seeing his work against the background of such figures as Feuerbach, Marx, Engels, Stirner, Trendelenburg and others who carried on the critique of the Hegelian system. One must be content, here, to remark that like other

Hegelians of the left, notably Marx and Engels, he developed a horror of the Hegelian concept of the mediatorial role of thought and strongly emphasized the importance of practical activity in arriving at *and making* the truth. The contrast between him, Marx, Engels, and Stirner in this regard, however, is one of the most fascinating object-lessons in the development of thought which limitations of space do not permit us to discuss.[24]

Finally: it does not seem possible to conclude this Foreword without an observation on the strange turns which History plays with men and events. Consider the principal dates associated with *The Point of View*—1859, the year when the work was first published, and 1848, the year when it was written. Both dates recall publications which revolutionized the worlds of thought and experience: the former, the *Origin of Species*, by a retiring British botanist, Charles Darwin; the latter, *The Communist Manifesto*, by Karl Marx and Friedrich Engels, Kierkegaard's fellow auditor—along with Bakunin, Herzen, Feuerbach and other notable figures—of Schelling's Berlin lectures in 1841.

Is it not odd that we look to this melancholy and splenetic Dane, who seemed to so many of his forward-looking contemporaries a 'misanthropic traitor against mankind', to be a foremost champion in the defense against the perversions of thought and existence which have been sired by the humanitarian spokesmen for 'scientific eugenics' and 'scientific socialism'?

Kierkegaard's *Point of View* tells us little about natural selection or the evolution of species, or of the destiny of the proletariat. He writes as an individual to 'the individual' about the responsibility of each of us every moment of his existence. Through the quirks of fate it is Kierkegaard's 'obscurantist' appeal which today sustains 'individuals' in the Sisyphean struggle against the blights of scientism and totalitarianism. To escape the shame of 1984 we need to renew ourselves again and again in the churning waters of Kierkegaard's *Point of View*.

BENJAMIN NELSON

NOTES

1. See below, pp. 50–51.

2. *Ibid.*, pp. 72–73.

3. *Ibid.*, p. 75.

4. *Ibid.*, p. 87.

5. See, especially: Walter Lowrie's 'long' biography of Kierkegaard, now available in a two-volume paperbound edition (New York: Harper Torchbooks, 1962) and Lee M. Capel's handy listing of works by and about Kierkegaard in the Appendix to the new printing; Aage Henriksen, *Methods and Results of Kierkegaard Studies in Scandinavia* (Copenhagen: Ejnar Munksgaard, 1951). The latter work has an instructive summary of full-length studies of Kierkegaard by Scandinavian psychiatrists.

6. See below, p. 132; cf. esp. *The Present Age* (New York: Oxford University Press, 1940) and *Concluding Unscientific Postscript* (Princeton: Princeton University Press, 1941).

7. Leading current commentators are agreed that an alternate phrase, 'sphere of existence', would reduce the risks of confusion in the understanding of Kierkegaard's notion of the three 'stages of life', the aesthetic, ethical, and religious. Particularly helpful discussions will be found in Regis Jolivet, *Introduction to Kierkegaard* (New York: Dutton, 1952) and James Collins, *The Mind of Kierkegaard* (Chicago: Regnery, 1953).

8. The above statement deliberately expands Kierkegaard's compressed way of referring to three 'stages' in the hope of facilitating the general and consistent use of this schema as a paradigm for the understanding of the varieties of human orientations to all possible objects of interest. The congruence between our remarks above and Kierkegaard's trichotomy should be evident.

9. For the contrasting evaluations of Kierkegaard's relation to Socrates, see the survey of the works of A. B. Drachmann, Vilhelm Andersen, Jens Himmelstrup and others in Aage Henriksen, *op. cit.*, esp. at pp. 131–38. Lee M. Capel is now completing a translation and study of Kierkegaard's *Concept of Irony* (1841), which is centered on the life and thought of Socrates. A detailed study of the place of Socrates in the imagination of nineteenth and twentieth century philosophers is a desideratum of contemporary research, but see A. W. Levi's preliminary paper on this theme, 'The Idea of Socrates: the philosophic hero in the nineteenth century', in the *Journal of the History of Ideas*, Vol. XVII (1956), pp. 89–108.

10. See the succinct discussion in Howard and Edna Hong's introduction to their new translation of Kierkegaard's *Works of Love* (New York: Harper, 1962).

11. Except for the two last terms, which name the central themes of Kierkegaard's *Repetition*, the phrases indicated above are sharply etched in *The Point of View*.

12. Kierkegaard had warned: 'Even for a martyr to accomplish anything in these times he must possess reflection, in order to so intrigue the age that it cleaves to him even when it puts him to death—that thus the awakening may follow.' See below, p. 90; for Kierkegaard's reference to himself as 'an absent one', cf. p. 99.

13. For an older summary of the principle approaches, which still applies in the main, see Henriksen, *Methods and Results*, pp. 10–12.

14. I am indebted to Mr. Lee M. Capel for a series of personal communications bearing on the untranslated passages in the *Journal*.

15. See R. Jolivet, *Introduction to Kierkegaard*, p. 225, and the entire chapter entitled 'Profit and Loss', pp. 219–38.

16. Preliminary indications of the backgrounds and meanings of the Redemption Disputes will be found in the present writer's *The Idea of Usury* (Princeton, 1949), esp. p. 144 n.

17. *The Merchant of Venice*, iv. 1. 199–200.

18. See below, p. 160.

19. See below, p. 90; cf. pp. 146–47 in notes.

20. See below, p. 161.

21. See W. Lowrie, *Kierkegaard* (New York: Harper Torchbooks, 1962), II, 605–18; also Dr. Lowrie's introduction to his translation of Kierkegaard's *Attack upon Christendom* (Boston: Beacon Press, 1956).

22. Henriksen summarizes the situation poignantly: 'It will appear from these examples that whether or not we follow Søren Kierkegaard's directions, we shall have reason to regret both procedures. A point of view which neither violates the totality nor the separate parts does not seem to have been attained by anybody. The core has not been penetrated.' *Op. cit.*, p. 10.

23. K. Loewith, *Von Hegel bis Nietzsche* (Stuttgart: Kohlhammer, 1941), *passim*.

24. Our own day has witnessed an extraordinary resurgence of the issues which were critical in the 1840's. Thus, there is much less novelty than first appears—indeed, the echo of the 1840's sounds everywhere—in the current debates (half-philosophical, half-political) over the relations of Hegelian dialectic (and phenomenology), existentialism, neo-Marxism, and pragmatism. The following developments are redolent with historical reminiscences:

TORCHBOOK PREFACE

No less a representative of American philosophy than Professor Sidney Hook has insisted that John Dewey anticipates whatever is valuable in the 'pragmatist core' of Heidegger's thought. Approaching a related question from another direction, leading French and Polish philosophers are emphasizing the need to supplement Marxism with humanist existentialism. Latterly, Erich Fromm has acclaimed that early Marx was the true pioneer of existentialism, adding that Marx's aversion to 'subject-object splits' reveals his affinity with Zen Buddhism! (*Marx's Concept of Man*. New York: Ungar, 1961). The wider public interested in deepening their understanding of such issues will be aided greatly by a close study of the neglected classics of the 1840's, many of which have become generally available in translation only during the last five years. It would help, also, if professional philosophers of every stamp would increase their familiarity with Kierkegaard's writings. Everyone loses when the 'Master of Irony' is consigned without ado to the irrationalists.

INTRODUCTION

by

WALTER LOWRIE

CONSIDERING the candour of the author's self-revelation, the ardour of his effort to make himself understood, and the pains he took to understand himself, *The Point of View* clearly belongs to the distinctive category of Christian writings which was first represented by the *Confessions* of St. Augustine. And yet it cannot aptly be called a confession, for S. K. refers to his *vita ante acta* only to exclude it from the report. His aim was to reveal the significance of his works, and he revealed himself only in so far as this aim required him to do so. And though we may compare this work with Newman's *Apologia pro vita sua*, we must beware of calling it an apology, even in the Latin sense of the word; for this is a description S. K. repudiates in these pages. It is true that, mindful of Xenophon's *Apology*, he first thought of using this title; but he promptly rejected it when he remembered that Socrates himself refused to use the apology a friendly orator had prepared for him. When he essayed for the first time to explain the purpose and purport of his works by describing his 'position as a Christian writer in Christendom', he proposed to entitle it 'Armed Neutrality'; but even the word 'neutrality' does not suffice to make this title sound pacific.

Moreover, this work, though it is profoundly autobiographical and is of inestimable value to a biographer of S. K., falls far short of being a biography and (in addition to the three longer notes in the Appendix) a brief sketch of his life may here be of use.

S. K. was born in Copenhagen on 5 May 1813, the youngest child of an elderly father who, coming as a poor peasant boy to the city, had acquired considerable wealth as a merchant and had retired from business to brood over his sins. The father was a man of strong character, with considerable intellectual ability, who brought up his children sternly in the fear of God.

In *The Point of View* S. K. says enough about his 'crazy upbringing' as a child. But the period of his youth, and the ten years passed in the university, he barely refers to as his *vita ante acta*, with the mere hint that he walked, alas, 'even in the path of perdition'. In fact, he lived for several years a disorderly life, in revolt against his father and against God. A gradual return in the direction of 'his old home' (i.e. the Christian position) culminated, on his twenty-fifth birthday, 5 May 1837 (when according to Danish law he attained majority), in a thorough reconciliation with his father, which was followed a few days later (19 May at 10.30 a.m.) by a very striking and effectual experience of conversion, which he speaks of in his *Journal* as an 'indescribable joy'. His father died soon after, leaving him a considerable fortune. Thereupon, largely out of deference to his father's wish, he began to apply himself seriously to the study of theology, the faculty in which he had long been inscribed, and two years later he passed his examination *cum laude*. He never became a pastor, yet almost to the end of his life he thought of this as a possibility and cherished it as an ideal.

No sooner had he taken his examination than he began to woo Regina Olsen (see note A in the Appendix). But during the tragic period of his engagement he was still a student in the university, working for the degree of Master of Arts (corresponding then to the doctorate in philosophy), and he won this degree on 29 September 1841, by his able dissertation on 'The Concept of Irony'. Twelve days later occurred the final breach with Regina, and to escape the scandal of it he retreated to Berlin to pursue his studies in philosophy. What really absorbed him, however, was an irresistible impulse to write. Regina, he said, had made him a poet. From that moment begins his tireless activity as an author. The documents here translated give a sufficient account of the period of authorship down to the end of the year 1848. During this period the only external events which affected him profoundly were the affair of the *Corsair* (see note B), which is often alluded to in these documents, and the political events of 1848 (see note C).

After S. K. had written this 'Explanation' of his life and work he had only six more years to live. These years were marked by intense insistence upon his religious aims of 'introducing Christianity into Christendom', culminating in the violent pamphleteering attack upon established Christianity, 'especially in Protestantism, and more especially in Denmark'. In the midst of this he was stricken with paralysis and died in a public hospital, wellnigh penniless, but with the consoling assurance that at last he had had the courage to live and die as a 'witness for the truth'. He had no more need to protest, as he does in *The Point of View*, that he was a religious writer, for it had become only too evident that he was that and nothing else.

I do not propose to explain here the characteristic expressions S. K. uses in these documents to express his original thoughts. I have taken pains to explain them in the Appendix of my work on *Kierkegaard*, but I recognize that they will not be adequately explained until many students have been enlisted in this effort. Not all of his most characteristic terms appear in these documents, for here he is solely intent upon emphasizing the religious categories: the contrast between the 'aesthetic' (eudaimonistic) and the religious points of view; the concept of the individual; the notion of divine providence; indirect communication (which he defends here lamely because he had already detected the daimonia which lurks in it); the absoluteness of the Christian claim, &c., &c. So here he all but ignores the profound psychological concepts which he had presented in his pseudonymous works. The 'Explanation' therefore, is very far from being an explanation of the Works as a whole.

THE POINT OF VIEW FOR MY WORK AS AN AUTHOR

A REPORT TO HISTORY

By

S. KIERKEGAARD

Written in 1848
*Published in Copenhagen in 1859 (four years after the
author's death) by his brother P. Chr. Kierkegaard.*

In everything the purpose must weigh with the folly.

SHAKESPEARE: Henry IV, Part II, ii. 2

What shall I say? My words alone
Do not express my duty.
O God, how great thy wisdom is,
Thy goodness, might and beauty.

BRORSON.

INTRODUCTION

IN my career as an author, a point has now been reached where it is permissible to do what I feel a strong impulse to do and so regard as my duty— namely, to explain once for all, as directly and frankly as possible, what is what: what I as an author declare myself to be. The moment (however unpropitious it may be in another sense) is now appropriate; partly because (as I have said) this point has been reached, and partly because I am about to encounter for the second time in the literary field my first production, *Either/Or*, in its second edition, which I was not willing to have published earlier.

There is a time to be silent and a time to speak. So long as I considered the strictest silence my religious duty I strove in every way to preserve it. I have not hesitated to counteract, in a *finite* sense, my own effort by the enigmatic mystery and *double entente* which silence favours. What I have done in that way has been misunderstood, has been explained as pride, arrogance, and God knows what. So long as I considered silence my religious duty I would not do the least thing to obviate such a misunderstanding. But the reason I considered silence my duty was that the authorship was not yet at hand in so complete a form that the understanding of it could be anything but misunderstanding.

The contents of this little book affirm, then, what I truly am as an author, that I am and was a religious author, that the whole of my work as an author is related to Christianity, to the problem 'of becoming a Christian', with a direct or indirect polemic against the monstrous illusion we call Christendom, or against the illusion that in such a land as ours all are Christians of a sort.

I would beg of every one who has the cause of Christianity at heart—and I beg the more urgently the more seriously he takes it to heart—that he make himself acquainted with this little book, not curiously, but devoutly, as one would read a religious work. How far a so-called aesthetic public has found or may find enjoyment in reading, attentively or casually, the productions of an aesthetic character, which are an incognito and a deceit in the service of Christianity, is naturally a matter of indifference to me; for I am a religious writer. Supposing that such a reader understands perfectly and appraises critically the individual aesthetic productions, he will nevertheless totally misunderstand me, inasmuch as he does not understand the religious totality in my whole work as an author. Suppose, then, that another understands my works in the totality of their religious reference, but does not understand a single one of the aesthetic productions contained in them—I would say that this lack of understanding is not an essential lack.

What I write here is for orientation. It is a public attestation; not a defence or an apology. In this respect, truly, if in no other, I believe that I have something in common with Socrates. For when he was accused, and was about to be judged by 'the crowd', his daemon forbade him to *defend* himself. Indeed, if he had done that, how unseemly it would have been, and how self-contradictory! Likewise there is something in me, and in the dialectical position I occupy, which makes it impossible for me, and impossible in itself, to conduct a defence for my work as an author. I have put up with a great deal, and I hope to put up with more without suffering the loss of my self—but who knows? perhaps the future will deal more gently with me than the past. The only thing I cannot put up with—cannot do so without suffering the loss of my self and of the dialectical character of my position (which is just what I cannot put up with)—this only thing is to *defend* myself *qua* author. That would be a falsehood, which, even though it were to help me finitely to gain the whole world, would eternally be my destruction. With humility before God, and also before men, I well know wherein I personally may have offended; but I know also with God that this very work of mine as an author was the prompting of an irresistible inward impulse, a melancholy man's only possibility, the honest effort on the part of a soul deeply humbled and penitent to do something by way of compensation, without shunning any sacrifice or labour in the service of truth. Therefore I know also with God, in whose eyes this undertaking found favour and still finds it, as it rejoices also in His assistance, that with regard to my authorship it is not I that need to defend myself before my contemporaries; for, if in this case I have any part, it is not as counsel for the defence but as prosecutor.

Yet I do not indict my contemporaries, seeing that I have religiously understood it as my duty thus to

7

serve the truth in self-denial, and as my task to do everything to prevent myself becoming esteemed and idolized. Only the man who knows in his own experience what true self-denial is can solve my riddle and perceive that it is self-denial. For the man who in himself has no experience of it must rather call my behaviour self-love, pride, eccentricity, madness—for which opinion it would be unreasonable of me to indict him, since I myself in the service of the truth have contributed to form it.[1] There is one thing unconditionally which cannot be understood either by a noisy assembly, or by a 'highly esteemed public', or in half an hour—and that one thing is the character of true Christian self-denial. To understand this requires fear and trembling, silent solitude, and a long interval of time.

That I have understood the truth which I deliver to others, of that I am eternally certain. And I am just as certain that my contemporaries, in so far as they do not understand it, will be compelled, whether by fair means or foul, to understand it some time, in eternity, when they are exempted from many distracting cares and troubles, from which I have been exempted. I have suffered under much misunderstanding; and the fact that I voluntarily exposed myself to it does not indicate that I am insensible to *real* suffering. As well deny the reality of all Christian suffering, for the mark of it is that it is voluntary. Neither does it follow as a matter of course and as a direct inference that 'the others' have no blame, seeing that it is in the service of truth I suffer this. But however much I have suffered from misunderstanding, I cannot but thank

8

God for what is of infinite importance to me, that He has granted me understanding of the truth.

And then only one thing more. It goes without saying that I cannot explain my work as an author wholly, i.e. with the purely personal inwardness in which I possess the explanation of it. And this in part because I cannot make public my God-relationship. It is neither more nor less than the generic human inwardness which every man may have, without regarding it as an official distinction which it were a crime to hide and a duty to proclaim, or which I could appeal to as my legitimation. In part because I cannot wish (and no one can desire that I might) to obtrude upon any one what concerns only my private person—though naturally there is much in this which for me serves to explain my work as an author.

PART ONE

A

THE AMBIGUITY OR DUPLICITY IN THE WHOLE AUTHORSHIP:* AS TO WHETHER THE AUTHOR IS AN AESTHETIC OR A RELIGIOUS AUTHOR

IT remains, then, to be shown that there is such a duplicity from first to last. This is not an instance of the common case where the assumed duplicity is discovered by some one else and the person concerned is obliged to prove that it *does not exist*. Not that at all, but quite the contrary. In case the reader should not be sufficiently observant of the duplicity, it is the business of the author to make as evident as possible the fact that it is there. That is to say, the duplicity, the ambiguity, is a conscious one, something the author knows more about than anybody else; it is the essential dialectical distinction of the whole authorship, and has therefore a deeper reason.

But is this a fact, is there such a pervading duplicity? May one not explain the phenomenon in another way, by supposing that there is an author who first was an aesthetic author, and then in the course of years

* In order that the titles of the books may be readily available they are given here. First group (aesthetic work): *Either/Or*; *Fear and Trembling*; *Repetition*; *The Concept of Dread*; *Prefaces*; *Philosophical Fragments*; *Stages on Life's Road*—along with eighteen edifying discourses which were published successively. Second group: *Concluding Unscientific Postscript*. Third group (religious works): *Edifying Discourses in Divers Spirits*; *The Works of Love*; *Christian Discourses*—along with a little aesthetic article, *The Crisis and a Crisis in the Life of an Actress*.

10

changed and became a religious author? I will not dwell upon the consideration that, if this were the case, the author would not have written such a book as the present one, and surely would hardly have undertaken to give a survey of the whole work—least of all would he have chosen the moment which coincides with the republication of his first book. Neither will I dwell upon the fact that it would be strange if such a change were to be accomplished in the course of only a few years. In other instances where an author originally aesthetic becomes a religious author, it is usual for many years to elapse, so that the hypothesis which explains the change by pointing to the fact that he has actually become considerably older does not lack plausibility. But this I will not dwell upon; for though it might seem strange and almost inexplicable, though it might prompt one to seek and find any other explanation, nevertheless it would not be absolutely impossible for such a change to occur in the space of only three years. I will show rather that it is impossible to explain the phenomenon in this way. For when one looks closer it will be seen that nothing like three years elapsed before the change occurred, but that the change is simultaneous with the beginning—that is, the duplicity dates from the very start. For the *Two Edifying Discourses* are contemporaneous with *Either/Or*. The duplicity in the deeper sense, that is, in the sense of the authorship as a whole, is not at all what was a subject of comment in its time, viz. the contrast between the two parts of *Either/Or*. No, the duplicity is discovered by comparing *Either/Or* and the *Two Edifying Discourses*.

The religious is present from the beginning. Conversely, the aesthetic is present again at the last moment. After two years, during which religious works only were published, there follows a little aesthetic article.* Hence assurance was provided both first and last against an interpretation of the phenomenon which supposes an aesthetic author who with the lapse of time has changed and become a religious author. Just as the *Two Edifying Discourses* came out between two and three months after *Either/Or*, so this little aesthetic article came out between two and three months after the purely religious writings of the two years. The *Two Edifying Discourses* and the little article correspond to one another conversely and prove conversely that the duplicity is both first and last. Although *Either/Or* attracted all the attention, and nobody noticed the *Two Edifying Discourses*, this book betokened, nevertheless, that the edifying was precisely what must come to the fore, that the author was a religious author, who for this reason has never written anything aesthetic, but has employed pseudonyms for all the aesthetic works, whereas the *Two Edifying Discourses* were by Magister Kierkegaard. Conversely, although the purely edifying works produced during the two years have possibly attracted the notice of others, no one, perhaps, in a deeper sense, has remarked upon the significance of the little article, which indicates that now the whole dialectical structure of the authorship is completed. The little article serves as a testimony in the confrontation of

* *The Crisis and a Crisis in the Life of an Actress*, in the *Fatherland* for July 1848.

witnesses, in order to make it impossible at the end (as the *Two Edifying Discourses* did at the beginning) to explain the phenomenon by supposing that there was an author who first was an aesthetic author and later *changed* and became subsequently a religious author—for he was a religious author from the beginning and was aesthetically productive even at the last moment.

The first group of writings represents aesthetic productivity, the last group is exclusively religious: between them, as the turning-point, lies the *Concluding Postscript*. This work concerns itself with and sets 'the Problem', which is the problem of the whole authorship: how to become a Christian. So it takes cognizance of the pseudonymous work, and of the eighteen edifying discourses as well, showing that all of this serves to illuminate the Problem—without, however, affirming that this was the aim of the foregoing production, which indeed could not have been affirmed by a pseudonym, a third person, incapable of knowing anything about the aim of a work which was not his own. The *Concluding Postscript* is not an aesthetic work, but neither is it in the strictest sense religious. Hence it is by a pseudonym, though I add my name as editor—a thing I did not do in the case of any purely aesthetic work.* This is a hint for him who is concerned about such things and has a flair for them. Then came the two years during which

* The *Literary Review* of the 'Two Generations' is no exception; partly because it is not aesthetic in the sense of poetic production, but is critical; and partly because it has a wholly religious background in the interpretation of 'the present age'.

13

nothing but religious works came out, all bearing my name. The period of the pseudonyms was past, the religious author had developed himself out of the aesthetic disguise—and then, as a testimony and as a precaution, came the little aesthetic article by a pseudonym, *Inter et Inter*. This is calculated to make one conscious all at once of the authorship as a whole. As I have remarked, it reminds one inversely of the *Two Edifying Discourses*.

THE EXPLANATION

That the Author is and was a Religious Author

IT might seem that a mere protestation to this effect on the part of the author himself would be more than enough; for surely he knows best what is meant. For my part, however, I have little confidence in protestations with respect to literary productions and am inclined to take an objective view of my own works. If as a third person, in the role of a reader, I cannot substantiate the fact that what I affirm is so, and that it could not but be so, it would not occur to me to wish to win a cause which I regard as lost. If I were to begin *qua* author to protest, I might easily bring to confusion the whole work, which from first to last is dialectical.

So I cannot make any protestation—not at least before I have gone about in another way to make the explanation so evident that a protestation of the sort here contemplated would be entirely superfluous. When that has been accomplished, a protestation might be *permissible* as a lyrical satisfaction to me, in case I were to feel an impulse to make it, and it might be *required* as a religious duty. For *qua* man I may be justified in protesting, and it may be my religious duty to make a protestation. But this must not be confounded with authorship: *qua* author it does not avail much that I protest *qua* man that I have intended this or that. But everybody will admit that when one is able to show with respect to a phenomenon that it cannot be explained in any other way, and that in this particular way it can be explained in every detail, or that the explanation fits at every point, then this explanation is substantiated as evidently as it is ever possible to establish the correctness of an explanation.

But is there not a contradiction here? It was established in the foregoing section that the ambiguity was present up to the last, and in so far as this was successfully proved, it becomes impossible to prove what the explanation is; so that a declaration, a protestation, seems in this case to be the only means of releasing the dialectical tension and untying the knot. This reasoning appears to be *acute*, but really it is *sophistical*. In case a sophistical person should find it necessary in a given contingency to resort to a mystification, it would be perfectly natural for him to do it in such a way that the comical situation results that he can't get himself out of it. But this, too, is due to a lack of seriousness, which prompts him to fall in love with mystification for its own sake, instead of using it for a purpose. Hence when a mystification, a dialectical reduplication,[2] is used in the service of a serious purpose, it will be so used as merely to obviate a misunderstanding, or an over-hasty understanding, whereas all the while the true explanation is at hand and ready to be found by him who honestly seeks it. To take the highest example: the whole life of Christ on earth would have been mere play if He had been incognito to such a degree that He went through life totally unnoticed—and yet in a true sense He was incognito.

So it is in the case of a dialectical reduplication; and

the mark of a dialectical reduplication is that the ambiguity is maintained. As soon as the requisite seriousness grasps it, it is able also to release it, but always in such a way that seriousness itself vouches for the fact of it. For as a woman's coyness has a reference to the true lover and yields when he appears, but only then, so, too, dialectical reduplication has a reference to true seriousness. To one less serious the explanation cannot be imparted, for the elasticity of the dialectical reduplication is too great for him to grasp: it takes the explanation away from him again and makes it doubtful to him whether it really is the explanation.

Let the attempt be made. Let us try to explain the whole of this literary production on the assumption that it was written by an aesthetic author. It is easy to perceive that from the beginning it is incongruous with this explanation, which breaks down when it encounters the *Two Edifying Discourses.* If, on the contrary, one will experiment with the assumption that it is a religious author, one will perceive that, step by step, the assumption corresponds at every point. The only thing that remains inexplicable is how it could occur to a religious author to employ aesthetics in such a way. That is to say, we are confronted again by the ambiguity or the dialectical reduplication. Only the difference now is that the assumption of his being a religious author will have taken firm hold, and it remains only to explain the ambiguity. How far it may be possible for a third person to do this I do not venture to determine; but the explanation is that contained in the Second Part of this little book.

Here only one thing more—a thing which, as I have said, may be a lyrical satisfaction to me *qua* man, and *qua* man is my religious duty; namely, a direct protestation that the author is and was a religious author. When I began *Either/Or* (of which, be it said parenthetically, there existed beforehand literally only about a page, viz. a few Diapsalmata, whereas the whole book was written in the space of eleven months, and the Second Part first) I was potentially as deeply under the influence of religion as ever I have been. I was so deeply shaken[A] that I understood perfectly well that I could not possibly succeed in striking the comforting and secure *via media* in which most people pass their lives: I had either to cast myself into perdition and sensuality, or to choose the religious absolutely as the only thing—either the world in a measure that would be dreadful, or the cloister. That it was the second I would and must choose was at bottom already determined: the eccentricity of the first movement[3] was merely the expression for the intensity of the second; it expressed the fact that I had become thoroughly aware how impossible it would be for me to be religious only up to a certain point. Here is the place of *Either/Or*. It was a poetical catharsis, which does not, however, go farther than the ethical. Personally, I was very far from wishing to summon the course of existence to return comfortingly to the situation of marriage for my sake, who religiously was already in the cloister—a thought which lies concealed in the pseudonym *Victor—Eremita*.

Such is the situation; strictly speaking, *Either/Or* was written in a monastery, and I can assure the reader (the assurance being especially addressed, if it should chance to fall under his eyes, to him who has no capacity or leisure to survey such a productivity as mine, yet has possibly been disturbed by the strange amalgamation of the religious and the aesthetic in my writings)—I can assure the reader that the author of *Either/Or* devoted a definite time every day, regularly and with monastic precision, to reading for his own sake edifying books, and that in fear and in much trembling he reflected upon his responsibility. Among other things, he reflected especially (how wonderful!) upon 'The Diary of the Seducer'. And then what occurred? The book had an immense success—especially (how wonderful!) 'The Diary of the Seducer'. The world opened its arms in an extraordinary way to the admired author, whom all this, however, did not 'seduce'—for he was an eternity too old for that.

Then followed *Two Edifying Discourses*—things of the most vital importance often seem insignificant. The big work, *Either/Or*, which was 'much read and more discussed'—and then the *Two Edifying Discourses*, dedicated to my deceased father, published on my birthday (May 5th), 'a little flower hidden in the great forest, not sought out either for its beauty, or for its scent, or because it was nourishing'.* No one took serious notice of the two discourses or concerned himself about them. Indeed I remember even that one of my acquaintances came to me with the complaint that in good faith he had gone and bought the book with the notion that, since it was by me, it must be something witty and clever. I remember, too, that

* Cf. the Preface to the *Two Edifying Discourses* of 1843.

I promised him, that if he wished, he should get his money back. I held out *Either/Or* to the world in my left hand, and in my right the *Two Edifying Discourses*; but all, or as good as all, grasped with their right what I held in my left.*

I had made up my mind before God what I should do: I staked my case on the *Two Edifying Discourses*; but I understood perfectly that only very few understood them.† And here for the first time comes in the category 'that *individual* whom with joy and gratitude I call *my* reader', a stereotyped formula which was repeated in the Preface to every collection of Edifying Discourses. No one can justly lay it to my charge that I have changed, that perhaps at a later moment, perhaps for the reason that I was not in the good graces of the public, I judged differently about this matter than I had before. No. If ever I stood in the good graces of the public, it was two or three months after the publication of *Either/Or*. And this very situation,

---

* Cf. the Preface to the *Two Edifying Discourses* of 1844: 'It seeks *my* reader, who receives in his right hand what is offered with the left.'

† Hence the tone of sadness in the Preface where it is said of the little book: 'Inasmuch as it may be said in a figurative sense that on its publication it starts out as it were upon a journey, I let my eye follow it a little while. I saw then how it went its way along lonely paths, or alone on the highways. After one or other little misunderstanding, due to the fact that it was deceived by a casual likeness, it finally encountered that individual whom with joy and gratitude I call *my* reader, whom it seeks, to whom as it were it stretches out its arms', &c. Cf. the Preface to the *Two Edifying Discourses* of 1843. This first Preface had and still has for me a very intimate and personal significance, such as it would hardly be possible for me to communicate.[4]

which to many perhaps would be a temptation, I regarded as the one favourable moment for doing what I had to do to assert my position, and I employed it in the service of the truth to introduce my category 'the individual'—it was then that I broke with the public, not out of pride and arrogance, &c. (and certainly not because at that moment the public was unfavourable to me, since on the contrary it was entirely favourable), but because I was conscious of being a religious author and as such was concerned with 'the individual' ('the individual'—in contrast to 'the public'), a thought in which is contained an entire philosophy of life and of the world.

From now on, that is, as early as the publication of *Fear and Trembling*, the serious observer who himself disposes of religious presuppositions, the serious observer to whom it is possible to make oneself intelligible at a distance, and to whom one can talk in silence (cf. the pseudonym Johannes—*de silentio*), was in a position to discern that this, after all, was a very singular sort of aesthetic production. And this was justly emphasized by the most reverend signature Kts., which delighted me greatly.*

* [*Note by the translator.* 'Kts.' was the signature which Bishop Mynster, the Primate of Denmark, commonly attached to his critical articles in the press.]

PART TWO

The Whole Work of Authorship construed from the point of view that the author is a religious author

CHAPTER I

A. THE AESTHETIC WORKS

Why the beginning of the work was aesthetic, or what this signifies, understood in relation to the whole*

§ 1

That 'Christendom' is a prodigious illusion.

EVERY one with some capacity for observation, who seriously considers what is called Christendom, or the conditions in a so-called Christian country, must surely be assailed by profound misgivings. What does it mean that all these thousands and thousands call themselves Christians as a matter of course? These many, many men, of whom the greater part, so far as one can judge, live in categories quite foreign to Christianity! Any one can convince himself of it by the simplest observation. People who perhaps never once enter a church, never think about God, never mention His name except in oaths! People upon whom it has never dawned that they might have any obligation to God, people who either regard it as a maximum to be guiltless of transgressing the criminal law, or do not count even this quite necessary! Yet all these people, even

* Once and for all I must earnestly beg the kind reader always to bear *in mente* that the thought behind the whole work is: what it means to become a Christian.

those who assert that no God exists, are all of them
Christians, call themselves Christians, are recognized
as Christians by the State, are buried as Christians by
the Church, are certified as Christians for eternity!

That at the bottom of this there must be a tremendous confusion, a frightful illusion, there surely can be
no doubt. But to stir up such a question! Yes, I know
the objections well. For there are those who understand what I mean, but would say with a good-natured
slap on the back, 'My dear fellow, you are still rather
young to want to embark on such an undertaking, an
undertaking which, if it is to have any success at all,
will require at least half a score of well-trained missionaries; an undertaking which means neither more
nor less than proposing to reintroduce Christianity . . .
into Christendom. No, my dear fellow, let us be men;
such an undertaking is beyond your powers and mine.
It is just as madly ambitious as wanting to reform the
"crowd", with which no sensible person wants to mix.
To start such a thing is certain ruin.' Perhaps; but
though ruin were certain, it is certain also that no one
has learnt this objection from Christianity; for when
Christianity came into the world it was still more
definitely 'certain ruin' to start such a thing—and yet
it was started. And it is certain, too, that no one
learnt this objection from Socrates; for he mixed
with the 'crowd' and wanted to reform it.

This is roughly how the case stands. Once in a
while a parson causes a little hubbub from the pulpit,
about there being something wrong somewhere with
all these numerous Christians—but all those *to* whom
he is speaking are Christians, and those he speaks *about*

are not present. This is most appropriately described as a feigned emotion. Once in a while there appears a religious enthusiast:[5] he storms against Christendom, he vociferates and makes a loud noise, denouncing almost all as not being Christians—and accomplishes nothing. He takes no heed of the fact that an illusion is not an easy thing to dispel. Supposing now it is a fact that most people, when they call themselves Christians, are under an illusion—how do they defend themselves against an enthusiast? First and foremost, they do not bother about him at all, they do not so much as look at his book, they immediately lay it aside, *ad acta*; or, if he employs the living word, they go round by another street and do not hear him. As the next step, they spirit him out of the way by carefully defining the whole concept, and settle themselves securely in their illusion: they make him a fanatic, his Christianity an exaggeration—in the end he remains the only one, or one of the few, who is not seriously a Christian (for exaggeration is surely a lack of seriousness), whereas the others are all serious Christians.

No, an illusion can never be destroyed directly, and only by indirect means can it be radically removed. If it is an illusion that all are Christians—and if there is anything to be done about it, it must be done indirectly, not by one who vociferously proclaims himself an extraordinary Christian, but by one who, better instructed, is ready to declare that he is not a Christian at all.* That is, one must approach from behind the

---

* One may recall the *Concluding Unscientific Postscript*, the author of which, Johannes Climacus, declares expressly that he himself is not a Christian.

person who is under an illusion. Instead of wishing to have the advantage of being oneself that rare thing, a Christian, one must let the prospective captive enjoy the advantage of being the Christian, and for one's own part have resignation enough to be the one who is far behind him—otherwise one will certainly not get the man out of his illusion, a thing which is difficult enough in any case.

If then, according to our assumption, the greater number of people in Christendom only imagine themselves to be Christians, in what categories do they live? They live in aesthetic, or, at the most, in aesthetic-ethical categories.

Supposing then that a religious writer has become profoundly attentive to this illusion, Christendom, and has resolved to attack it with all the might at his disposal (with God's aid, be it noted)—what then is he to do? First and foremost, no impatience. If he becomes impatient, he will rush headlong against it and accomplish nothing. A direct attack only strengthens a person in his illusion, and at the same time embitters him. There is nothing that requires such gentle handling as an illusion, if one wishes to dispel it. If anything prompts the prospective captive to set his will in opposition, all is lost. And this is what a direct attack achieves, and it implies moreover the presumption of requiring a man to make to another person, or in his presence, an admission which he can make most profitably to himself privately. This is what is achieved by the indirect method, which, loving and serving the truth, arranges everything dialectically for the prospective captive, and then shyly withdraws (for love is always shy), so as not to witness the admission which he makes to himself alone before God—that he has lived hitherto in an illusion.

The religious writer must, therefore, first get into touch with men. That is, he must begin with aesthetic achievement. This is earnest-money. The more brilliant the achievement, the better for him. Moreover he must be sure of himself, or (and this is the one and only security) he must relate himself to God in fear and trembling, lest the event most opposite to his intentions should come to pass, and instead of setting the others in motion, the others acquire power over him, so that he ends by being bogged in the aesthetic. Therefore, he must have everything in readiness, though without impatience, with a view to bringing forward the religious promptly, as soon as he perceives that he has his readers with him, so that with the momentum gained by devotion to the aesthetic they rush headlong into contact with the religious.

It is important that religion should not be introduced either too soon or too late. If too long a time elapses, the illusion gains ground that the aesthetic writer has become older and hence religious. If it comes too soon, the effect is not violent enough.

Assuming that there is a prodigious illusion in the case of these many men who call themselves Christians and are regarded as Christians, the way of encountering it which is here suggested involves no condemnation or denunciation. It is a truly Christian invention, which cannot be employed without fear and trembling, or without real self-denial. The one who is disposed to help bears all the responsibility and makes all the effort. But for that reason such a line of action possesses intrinsic value. Generally speaking, a method has value only in relation to the result attained. Some one condemns and denounces, vociferates and makes a great noise—all this has no intrinsic value, though one counts upon accomplishing much by it. It is otherwise with the line of action here contemplated. Suppose that a man had dedicated himself to the use of it, suppose that he used it his whole life long—and suppose that he accomplished nothing: he has nevertheless by no means lived in vain, for his life was true self-denial.

§ 2

That if real success is to attend the effort to bring a man to a definite position, one must first of all take pains to find HIM where he is and begin there.

This is the secret of the art of helping others. Any one who has not mastered this is himself deluded when he proposes to help others. In order to help another effectively I must understand more than he— yet first of all surely I must understand what he understands. If I do not know that, my greater understanding will be of no help to him. If, however, I am disposed to plume myself on my greater understanding, it is because I am vain or proud, so that at bottom, instead of benefiting him, I want to be admired. But all true effort to help begins with self-humiliation: the helper must first humble himself under him he would help, and therewith must understand that to help does not mean to be a sovereign but to be a servant, that to help does not mean to be ambitious but to be patient, that to help means to endure for the time being the imputation that one is in the wrong and does not understand what the other understands.

Take the case of a man who is passionately angry, and let us assume that he is really in the wrong. Unless you can begin with him by making it seem as if it were he that had to instruct you, and unless you can do it in such a way that the angry man, who was too impatient to listen to a word of yours, is glad to discover in you a complaisant and attentive listener—if you cannot do that, you cannot help him at all. Or take the case of a lover who has been unhappy in love, and suppose that the way he yields to his passion is really unreasonable, impious, unchristian. In case you cannot begin with him in such a way that he finds genuine relief in talking to you about his suffering and is able to enrich his mind with the poetical interpretations you suggest for it, notwithstanding you have no share in this passion and want to free him from it—if you cannot do that, then you cannot help him at all; he shuts himself away from you, he retires within himself . . . and then you only prate to him. Perhaps by the power of your personality you may be able to coerce him to acknowledge that he is at fault. Ah! my dear, the next moment he steals away by a hidden path for a rendezvous with his hidden passion, for which he longs all the more ardently, and is almost fearful lest it might have lost something of its seductive warmth; for now by your behaviour you have helped him to fall in love all over again, in love now with his unhappy passion itself . . . and you only prate to him!

So it is with respect to what it means to become a Christian—assuming that the many who call themselves Christians are under an illusion. Denounce the magical charm of aesthetics—well, there have indeed been times when you might have succeeded in coercing people. But with what result? With the result that privately, with secret passion, they love that magic. No, let it come out. And remember, serious and stern as you are, that if you cannot humble yourself, you are not genuinely serious. Be the amazed listener who sits and hears what the other finds the more delight in telling you because you listen with amazement. But above all do not forget one thing, the purpose you have in mind, the fact that it is the religious you must bring forward. If you are capable of it, present the aesthetic with all its fascinating magic, enthral if possible the other man, present it with the sort of passion which exactly suits him, merrily for the merry, in a minor key for the melancholy, wittily for the witty, &c. But above all do not forget one thing, the purpose you have to bring forward . . . the religious. By all means do this, and fear not to do it; for truly it cannot be done without fear and trembling.

If you can do that, if you can find exactly the place where the other is and begin there, you may perhaps have the luck to lead him to the place where you are.

For to be a teacher does not mean simply to affirm that such a thing is so, or to deliver a lecture, &c. No, to be a teacher in the right sense is to be a learner.

Instruction begins when you, the teacher, learn from the learner, put yourself in his place so that you may understand what he understands and in the way he understands it, in case you have not understood it before. Or if you have understood it before, you allow him to subject you to an examination so that he may be sure you know your part. This is the introduction. Then the beginning can be made in another sense.

An objection I have constantly raised in my own mind against a class of the orthodox here at home[6] is that they shut themselves up in little groups and confirm one another in the belief that they are the only Christians—and therefore know of nothing else to do about Christendom as a whole but to vociferate that the others are nòt Christians. If it is true that there really are so very few Christians in Christendom, these orthodox people are *eo ipso* under obligation to be missionaries, although a missionary in Christendom will always look rather different from a missionary to the heathen. It will easily be perceived that this objection of mine attacks our orthodox in correct fashion, from behind; for it proceeds upon the admission, or the assumption, that they really are true Christians, the only true Christians in Christendom.

So then the religious writer, whose all-absorbing thought is how one is to become a Christian, starts off rightly in Christendom as an aesthetic writer. For a moment let it remain undetermined whether Christendom is a monstrous illusion, whether it is a vain conceit for the many to call themselves Christians; let the opposite rather be assumed. Well then, this beginning is a superfluity, counting upon a situation which does not exist—yet it does no harm. The harm is much greater, or rather the only harm is, when one who is not a Christian pretends to be one. On the other hand, when one who is a Christian gives the impression that he is not, the harm is not great. Assuming that all are Christians, this deception can at the most confirm them more and more in being such.

§ 3

The illusion that religion and Christianity are something one first has recourse to when one grows older.

The aesthetical always overrates youth and this brief instant of eternity. It cannot reconcile itself to the seriousness of age, let alone the seriousness of eternity. Hence the aesthete is always suspicious of the religious person, supposing either that he never had any feeling for aesthetics, or else that essentially he would have preferred to remain in the enjoyment of it, but that time exercised its debilitating influence, and he became older and took refuge in religion. Life is divided into two parts: the period of youth belongs to the aesthetical; the later age to religion—but, speaking honestly, we all would prefer to remain young.

How *may* this illusion be dispelled? I say 'may', for whether the effort actually succeeds is another question; but it may be dispelled by the simultaneous achievement of aesthetic and religious production. In this case no room is left for doubt, for the aesthetic production attests the fact of youth—and so the simultaneous achievement in the religious sphere cannot be explained upon any accidental ground.

Assuming that Christendom is a prodigious illusion, that it is a vain conceit for the many to call themselves Christians, there seems to be every probability that the illusion we are now talking about is exceedingly common. But this illusion is still farther aggravated by the conceit that one is a Christian. One lives in aesthetic categories, and if once in a while thoughts about Christianity occur, the question is deferred till one becomes older. 'For', one says to oneself, 'in fact I am essentially a Christian.' It certainly cannot be denied that in Christendom there are those who live just as sensually as ever any heathen did; yes, even more sensually, because they have this disastrous sense of security that essentially they are Christians. But the decision to become a Christian one shirks as long as possible; indeed one encounters an additional hindrance in the fact that one takes pride in being young as long as possible (and only when one grows old does one have recourse to Christianity and religiousness). Then one will be compelled to make the admission that one has become old—but only when one becomes old will one have recourse to Christianity and religiousness.

If one could always remain young, one would not have the least need either of Christianity or religion.

This is an error most pernicious to all true religiousness. It is rooted in the fact that people confuse the notion of growing older in the sense of time with that of growing older in the sense of eternity. It cannot indeed be denied that one not infrequently sees the unedifying spectacle of a youth who was the hot and passionate spokesman of aesthetics transformed into a type of religiousness which has all the faults of old age, in one sense feeble, in another too highly strung. It cannot be denied that many who represent the religious do so too sternly and too crabbedly, for fear of not being serious enough. This and much else may contribute to make the illusion more general and to establish it more firmly. But what help is there for it? The only help is what will help to dispel this illusion.

So if a religious author wishes to deal with this illusion, he must be at the same time an aesthetic and a religious author. But one thing above all he must not forget, the intention of the whole undertaking, that what must come decisively to the fore is the religious. The aesthetic works remain only a means of communication; and for those who possibly may need it (and on the assumption that Christendom is a prodigious illusion these must be many) it serves as a proof that it is impossible to explain the religious production by the notion that the author has become older; for it is in fact simultaneous, and surely one has not grown older simultaneously.

Perhaps success may not attend such an effort—perhaps, but at all events no great harm is done. The harm is, at the most, that some will not believe in the religiousness of such a communicator. All right then! A communicator of the religious may very often be over-anxious on his own behalf to be regarded as religious. If such be the case, it shows clearly that he is not truly a religious character. It is like the case of a teacher who is too much concerned about the judgement his pupils may pass upon his instruction, his knowledge, &c. Such a teacher when he tries to teach is unable to move hand or foot. Suppose, for example, he thought it best for his pupils' sake to say of something he understood quite well that he did not understand it. Good gracious! This he could not venture to do, for fear the pupils might really believe that he did not understand it. That is to say, he is not fit to be a teacher—though he calls himself a teacher, he is so far from being such a thing that he actually aspires to be cited for commendation . . . by his pupils. Or as in the case of a preacher of repentance who, when he wants to chastise the vices of the age, is much concerned about what the age thinks of him. He is so far from being a preacher of repentance that he resembles rather a New Year's visitor who comes with congratulations. He merely makes himself a bit interesting in a costume which is rather queer for a New Year's visitor. And so it is with the religious character who, if worse come to worst, cannot endure to be regarded as the only person who is not religious. For to be able to endure this is, in the sphere of reflection, the most accurate definition of essential religiousness.

§ 4

That even if a man will not follow where one endeavours to lead him, one thing it is still possible to do for him—compel him to take notice.

One man may have the good fortune to do much for another, he may have the good fortune to lead him whither he wishes, and (to stick to the subject which here is our constant and essential interest) he may have the good fortune to help him to become a Christian. But this result is not in my power; it depends upon so many things, and above all it depends upon whether he will or no. In all eternity it is impossible for me to compel a person to accept an opinion, a conviction, a belief. But one thing I can do: I can compel him to take notice. In one sense this is the first thing; for it is the condition antecedent to the next thing, i.e. the acceptance of an opinion, a conviction, a belief. In another sense it is the last—if, that is, he will not take the next step.

That this is a charitable act there can be no dispute, but it also must not be forgotten that it is a rash act. By obliging a man to take notice I achieve the aim of obliging him to judge. Now he is about to judge—but how he judges is not under my control. Perhaps he judges in the very opposite sense to that which I desire. Moreover, the fact that he was compelled to judge may perhaps have embittered him, furiously embittered him, against the cause and against me. And perhaps I am the victim of my rash act. Compelling people to take notice and to judge is the characteristic of genuine martyrdom. A genuine martyr never used his might but strove by the aid of impotence. He compelled people to take notice. God knows, they took notice—they put him to death. But with that he was well content. He did not count that his death put a stop to his work; he understood that his death was a part of it, indeed that his work first gained headway by means of his death. For verily those who put him to death took notice in their turn; they were compelled to consider the cause again, and to an entirely different effect. What the living man was unable to do, the dead man could—he won for his cause those who had taken notice.

There is an objection I have raised again and again in my own mind against the preachers we ordinarily find preaching Christianity in Christendom. Surrounded as they are by too much illusion and rendered secure by it, they have not the courage to make men take notice. That is to say, they are not sufficiently self-denying in view of their cause. They are glad to win adherents, but they want to win them for the sake of strengthening their cause, and so they do not inquire any too carefully whether they truly are adherents. Again, this means that in a deeper sense they have no cause. Their cause is one to which they are selfishly attached. Hence they do not venture to go out among men in a real sense, or to let go of the illusion for the sake of imparting an impression of the pure idea. They have an obscure apprehension that it is a dangerous thing to compel people in truth to take notice. In untruth to make people take notice—that is, to bow and scrape before them, to flatter them, to implore their attention and their indulgent judgement, to refer (the truth!) to the ballot—this indeed is not attended by any danger, at least not here on earth, where on the contrary it is attended with advantages of every sort. And yet perhaps it is also attended with the danger that some day, in eternity, one may be 'plucked'.

And now with reference to the assumption that it is a vain conceit on the part of the many who call themselves Christians. If a man lives in this conceit, lives, that is to say, in categories entirely foreign to Christianity, in purely aesthetic categories, and if some one is capable of winning and captivating him with aesthetic works, and then knows how to introduce the religious so promptly that with the momentum of his abandonment to the aesthetic the man rushes straight into the most decisive definitions of the religious—what then? Why, then, he must take notice. What follows after this, however, no one can tell beforehand. But at least he is compelled to take notice. Possibly he may come to his senses and realize what is implied in calling himself a Christian. Possibly he may be furious with the person who has taken this liberty with him; but at least he has begun to take notice, he is on the point of expressing a judgement. Possibly, in order to protect his retreat, he may express the judgement that the other is a hypocrite, a deceiver, a dunce—but there is no help for it, he must judge, he has begun to take notice.

Normally one reverses the relationship; and it was indeed reversed when Christianity dealt with paganism. But the fact that the situation was entirely altered by the notion of Christendom, which transposes everything into the sphere of reflection, is completely overlooked. In Christendom, the man who endeavours to lead people to become Christians normally gives every sort of assurance that he himself is a Christian. He protests and protests. But he fails to observe that from the very beginning there has been a terrible confusion at this point; for in fact the people he addresses are already Christians. But if it is

Christians he is addressing, what can be the sense of getting them to become Christians? If, on the contrary, they are not Christians, in his opinion, although they call themselves such, the very fact that they call themselves Christians shows that here we have to do with a situation which demands reflection, and with that the tactics must be entirely reversed.

Here I cannot develop further the pressing need Christendom has of an entirely new military science[7] permeated through and through by reflection. In several of my books I have furnished suggestions about the principal factors of such a science. The gist of it all can be expressed in *one* word: the method must be indirect. But the development of this method may require the labour of years, alert attention every hour of the day, daily practice of the scales, or patient finger-exercise in the dialectical, not to speak of a never-slumbering fear and trembling. In the communication of Christianity, where the situation is qualified by Christendom, there is no direct or straightforward relationship, inasmuch as a vain conceit has first to be disposed of. All the old military science, all the apologetic and whatever goes with it, serves rather —candidly speaking—to betray the cause of Christianity. At every instant and at every point the tactics must be adapted to a fight which is waged against a conceit, an illusion.

So then when a religious author in Christendom whose all-absorbing thought is the task of becoming a Christian would do all that he possibly can to make people take notice (for whether he succeeds or not is another question), he must begin as an aesthetic writer and up to a definite point he must maintain this role. But there is necessarily a limit; for the aim of it is to make people take notice. And one thing the author must not forget, namely, his purpose, the distinction between this and that, between the religious as the decisive thing and the aesthetic incognito—lest the criss-cross of dialectics end in twaddle.

§ 5

That the whole of the aesthetic work, viewed in relation to the work as a whole, is a deception—understanding this word, however, in a special sense.

Any one who considers the aesthetic work as the whole and then considers the religious part from this point of view, could only consider it as a falling away, a falling off. I have shown in the foregoing that the assumption upon which this point of view is based is not tenable. There it was established that from the very beginning, and simultaneously with the pseudonymous work, certain signals, displaying my name, gave telegraphic notice of the religious.

But from the point of view of my whole activity as an author, integrally conceived, the aesthetic work is a deception, and herein is to be found the deeper significance of the use of pseudonyms. A deception, however, is a rather ugly thing. To this I would make answer: One must not let oneself be deceived by the word 'deception'. One can deceive a person for the truth's sake, and (to recall old Socrates) one can deceive a person into the truth. Indeed, it is only by this means, i.e. by deceiving him, that it is possible to bring into the truth one who is in an illusion. Whoever rejects this opinion betrays the fact that he is not over-well versed in dialectics, and that is precisely what is especially needed when operating in this field. For there is an immense difference, a dialectical difference, between these two cases: the case of a man who is ignorant and is to have a piece of knowledge imparted to him, so that he is like an empty vessel which is to be filled or a blank sheet of paper upon which something is to be written; and the case of a man who is under an illusion and must first be delivered from that. Likewise there is a difference between writing on a blank sheet of paper and bringing to light by the application of a caustic fluid a text which is hidden under another text. Assuming then that a person is the victim of an illusion, and that in order to communicate the truth to him the first task, rightly understood, is to remove the illusion—if I do not begin by deceiving him, I must begin with direct communication. But direct communication presupposes that the receiver's ability to receive is undisturbed. But here such is not the case; an illusion stands in the way. That is to say, one must first of all use the caustic fluid. But this caustic means is negativity, and negativity understood in relation to the communication of the truth is precisely the same as deception.

What then does it mean, 'to deceive'? It means that one does not begin *directly* with the matter one wants to communicate, but begins by accepting the other man's illusion as good money. So (to stick to the theme with which this work especially deals) one does not begin thus: I am a Christian; you are not a Christian. Nor does one begin thus: It is Christianity I am proclaiming; and you are living in purely aesthetic categories. No, one begins thus: Let us talk about aesthetics. The deception consists in the fact that one talks thus merely to get to the religious theme. But, on our assumption, the other man is under the illusion that the aesthetic is Christianity; for, he thinks, I am a Christian, and yet he lives in aesthetic categories.

Although ever so many parsons were to consider this method unjustifiable, and just as many were unable to get it into their heads (in spite of the fact that they all of them, according to their own assertion, are accustomed to use the Socratic method), I for my part tranquilly adhere to Socrates. It is true, he was not a Christian; that I know, and yet I am thoroughly convinced that he has become one. But he was a dialectician, he conceived everything in terms of reflection. And the question which concerns us here is a purely dialectical one, it is the question of the use of reflection in Christendom. We are reckoning here with two qualitatively different magnitudes, but in a formal sense I can very well call Socrates my teacher— whereas I have only believed, and only believe, in One, the Lord Jesus Christ.

B. THE *CONCLUDING POSTSCRIPT*

Constitutes, as I have already said, the turning-point in my whole work as an author. It presents the 'Problem', that of becoming a Christian. Having appropriated the whole pseudonymous, aesthetic work as the description of *one* way a person may take to become a Christian (viz. *away* from the aesthetical in order to become a Christian), it undertakes to describe the other way (viz. *away* from the System, from speculation, &c., in order to become a Christian).

C. THE RELIGIOUS WORK

I could express myself very briefly even with regard to the *Concluding Postscript*, since that book does not present any difficulties when the point of view for the literary work as a whole is that the author is a religious author. The only thing that required explanation was the question how, on this assumption, the aesthetic work was to be conceived. And what, on this assumption, requires no explanation at all is the last section, the purely religious work, which of course establishes the point of view.

CONCLUSION

What does all this come to, when the reader puts together the points dwelt upon in the foregoing paragraphs? It means that this is a literary work in which the whole thought is the task of becoming a Christian. But it is a literary work which understood from the very first and consistently followed out the implication of the fact that the situation is Christendom—a reflective modification—and hence transformed into reflection all the relationships of Christianity. To become a Christian in Christendom means either to become what one is (the inwardness of reflection or to become inward through reflection), or it means that the first thing is to be disengaged from the toils of one's illusion, which again is a reflective modification. Here there is no room for vacillation or ambiguity of the sort one commonly experiences elsewhere when one does not know and cannot make out whether one is situated in paganism, whether the parson is a missionary in that sense, or whereabouts one is. Here one does not miss what is generally lacking, viz. a decisive categorical definition and a decisive expression for the situation: to preach Christianity . . . in Christendom. Everything is put in terms of reflection. The communication is qualified by reflection, hence it is indirect communication. The communicator is characterized by reflection, therefore he is negative—not one who says that he himself is a Christian in an extraordinary degree, or even lays claim to revelations[8] (all of which answers to immediacy and direct communication); but, on the contrary, one who even affirms that he is not a Christian. That is to say, the communicator stands behind the other man, helping him negatively—for whether he actually succeeds in helping some one is another question. The problem itself is a problem of reflection: to become a Christian . . . when one is a Christian of a sort.

CHAPTER II

THE DIFFERENCE IN MY PERSONAL MODE OF EXISTENCE CORRESPONDING TO THE ESSENTIAL DIFFERENCE IN THE WORKS

IN this age, and indeed for many ages past, people have quite lost sight of the fact that authorship is and ought to be a serious calling implying an appropriate mode of personal existence. They do not realize that the press in general, as an expression of the abstract and impersonal communication of ideas, and the daily press in particular, because of its formal indifference to the question whether what it reports is true or false, contributes enormously to the general demoralization, for the reason that the impersonal, which for the most part is irresponsible and incapable of repentance, is essentially demoralizing. They do not realize that anonymity, as the most absolute expression for the impersonal, the irresponsible, the unrepentant, is a fundamental source of the modern demoralization. On the other hand, they do not reflect that anonymity would be counteracted in the simplest possible way, and that a wholesome corrective would be furnished for the abstractness of printed communication, if people would but turn back again to antiquity and learn what it means to be a single individual man, neither more nor less—which surely even an author is too, neither more nor less. This is perfectly obvious. But in our age, which reckons as wisdom that which is truly the mystery of unrighteousness, viz. that one need not inquire about the communicator, but only about the communication, the objective only—in our age what is an author? An author is often merely an *x*, even when his name is signed, something quite impersonal, which addresses itself abstractly, by the aid of printing, to thousands and thousands, while remaining itself unseen and unknown, living a life as hidden, as anonymous, as it is possible for a life to be, in order, presumably, not to reveal the too obvious and striking contradiction between the prodigious means of communication employed and the fact that the author is only a single individual—perhaps also for fear of the control which in practical life must always be exercised over every one who wishes to teach others, to see whether his personal existence comports with his communication. But all this, which deserves the most serious attention on the part of one who would study the demoralization of the modern state—all this I cannot enter into more particularly here.

A. THE PERSONAL MODE OF EXISTENCE IN RELATION TO THE AESTHETIC WORKS

I come now to the first period of my authorship and my mode of existence. Here was a religious author, but one who began as an aesthetic author; and this first stage was one of incognito and deceit. Initiated as I was very early and very thoroughly into the secret that *Mundus vult decipi*, I was not in the position of being able to wish to follow such tactics. Quite the contrary. With me it was a question of deceiving inversely on the greatest possible scale, employing every bit of knowledge I had about men and their weaknesses and their stupidities, not to profit thereby, but to annihilate myself and weaken the impression I made. The secret of the deceit which suits the world which wants to be deceived consists partly in forming a coterie and all that goes with that, in joining one or another of those societies for mutual admiration, whose members support one another with tongue and pen in the pursuit of worldly advantage; and it consists partly in hiding oneself from the human crowd, never being seen, so as to produce a fantastic effect. So I had to do exactly the opposite. I had to exist in absolute isolation and guard my solitude, but at the same time take pains to be seen every hour of the day, living as it were upon the street, in company with Tom, Dick, and Harry, and in the most fortuitous situations. This is truth's way of deceiving, the everlastingly sure way of weakening, in a worldly sense, the impression one makes. It was, moreover, the way followed by men of a very different calibre from mine to make people take notice. Those reputable persons, the deceivers who want the communication to serve them instead of serving the communication, are on the look-out only to win repute for themselves. Those despised persons, the 'witnesses for the truth', who deceive inversely, have ever been wont to suffer themselves to be set at naught in a worldly sense and be counted as nothing—in spite of the fact that they labour day and night, and suffer besides from having no support whatever in the illusion that the work they perform is their career and their 'living'.

So this had to be done, and it was done, not now and then, but every day. I am convinced that one-sixth of *Either/Or*, together with a bit of coterie, and then an author who was never to be seen—especially if this was carried on for a considerable time—must make a much more extraordinary effect. I, however, had made myself sure of being able to work as laboriously as I pleased and as the spirit prompted me, without having to fear that I might get too much renown. For in a certain sense I was working as laboriously in another direction—against myself. Only an author will be able to understand what a task it is to work *qua* author, i.e. with mind and pen, and yet be at the beck and call of everybody. Although this mode of existence enriched me immensely with observations of human life, it is a standard of conduct which would bring most men to despair. For it means the effort to dispel every illusion and to present the idea in all its purity—and verily, it is not truth that rules the world but illusions. Even if a literary achievement were more illustrious than any that has yet been seen—if only the author were to live as is here suggested, he would in a brief time have insured himself against worldly renown and the crowd's brutish adulation. For the crowd possesses no idealism, and hence no power of retaining impressions in spite of contrary appearances. It is always the victim of appearances. To be seen again and again, and to be seen in the most fortuitous situations, is enough to make the crowd forget its first impression of the man and become soon sick and tired of him. And, after all, to keep oneself perpetually in view does not consume a great deal of time, if only one employs one's time shrewdly (i.e. in a worldly sense insanely) and to the best effect, by going back and forth past the same spot, and that the most frequented spot in the city. Every one who husbands his reputation, in a worldly sense, will not return by the same way he went, even if it is the most convenient way. He will avoid being seen twice in so short a time, for fear people might suppose he had nothing to do, whereas if he sat in his room at home three-quarters of the day and was idle, such a thought would never occur to anybody. On the other hand, an hour well spent, in a godly sense, an hour lived for eternity and spent by going back and forth among the common people . . . is not such a small thing after all. And verily it is well pleasing to God that the truth should be served in this way. His Spirit witnesseth mightily with my spirit[9] that it has the full consent of His Divine Majesty. All the witnesses of the truth indicate their approval, recognizing that one is disposed to serve the truth, the idea, and not to betray the truth and profit by the illusion. I experienced a real Christian satisfaction in venturing to perform on Monday a little bit of that which one weeps about on Sunday (when the parson prates about it and weeps too) . . . and on Monday one is ready to laugh about. I had real Christian satisfaction in the thought that, if there were no other, there was definitely one man in Copenhagen whom every poor man could freely accost and converse with on the street; that, if there were no other, there was one man who, whatever the society he more commonly frequented, did not shun contact with the poor, but greeted every maidservant he was acquainted with, every manservant, every common labourer. I felt a real Christian satisfaction in the fact that, if there were no other, there was one man who (several years before existence set the race another lesson to learn)[10] made a practical effort on a small scale to learn the lesson of loving one's neighbour and alas! got at the same time a frightful insight into what an illusion Christendom is, and (a little later,[11] to be sure) an insight also into what a situation the simpler classes suffered themselves to be seduced by paltry newspaper-writers, whose struggle or fight for equality (since it is in the service of a lie) cannot lead to any other result but to prompt the privileged classes in self-defence to stand proudly aloof from the common man, and to make the common man insolent in his forwardness.

The description of my personal existence cannot be carried out here in greater detail; but I am convinced that seldom has any author employed so much cunning, intrigue, and shrewdness to win honour and reputation in the world with a view to deceiving it, as I displayed in order to deceive it inversely in the interest of truth. On how great a scale this was carried out I shall attempt to show by one single instance, known to my friend Giødwad,[12] the proof-reader of *Either/Or*. I was so busy when I was reading the proofs of *Either/Or* that it was impossible to spend the usual time sauntering back and forth on the street. I did not get through the work till late in the evening, and then I hastened to the theatre, where I remained literally only from five to ten minutes. And why did I do this? Because I feared the big book would create

for me too great a reputation.* And why did I do this?
Because I knew human nature, especially in Copenhagen. To be seen every night for five minutes by
several hundred people sufficed to substantiate the
opinion: He hasn't the least thing in the world to do;
he is a mere idler.

Such was the existence I led by way of seconding
my aesthetic work. Incidentally it involved a breach
with all coteries. And I formed the polemical resolution to regard every eulogy as an attack, and every
attack as a thing unworthy of notice. Such was my
public mode of existence. I almost never made a visit,
and at home the rule was strictly observed to receive
no one except the poor who came to seek help. For I
had no time to receive visitors at home, and any one
who entered my home as a visitor might easily get a
presentiment of a situation about which he should
have no presentiment. Thus I existed. If Copenhagen ever has been of one opinion about anybody, I
venture to say that it was of one opinion about me,
that I was an idler, a dawdler, a *flâneur*, a frivolous
bird, intelligent, perhaps brilliant, witty, &c.—but as
for 'seriousness', I lacked it utterly. I represented a
worldly irony, *joie de vivre*, the subtlest form of
pleasure-seeking—without a trace of 'seriousness and

* It was for the same reason that at the moment when the
whole of *Either/Or* was ready to be transcribed into a fair
copy, I printed a little article in the *Fatherland* over my own
signature, in which I gratuitously disclaimed that I was the
author of a good many interesting articles which had appeared anonymously in various newspapers, acknowledging
and admitting my idleness, and making one petition, that
henceforth no one would ever regard me as the author of
anything beneath which my name was not signed.

positivity'; on the other hand, I was prodigiously witty and interesting.

When I look back upon that time, I am almost tempted to make some sort of apology to the people of importance and repute in the community. For true enough, I knew perfectly well what I was doing, yet from their standpoint they were right in finding fault with me, because by thus impairing my own prestige I contributed to the movement which was impairing power and renown in general—notwithstanding that I have always been conservative in this respect, and have found joy in paying to the eminent and distinguished the deference, awe, and admiration which are due to them. Yet my conservative disposition did not involve a desire to have this sort of distinction for myself. And just because the eminent and distinguished members of the community have shown me in so many ways not only sympathy but partiality, have sought in so many ways to draw me to their side (which certainly was honest and well-meant on their part)—just for this reason I feel impelled to make them an apology, although naturally I cannot regret what I have done, since I served my idea. People of distinction have always proved more consistent in their treatment of me than the simpler classes, who even from their own standpoint did not behave rightly, since they too (according to the foregoing account) attacked me[B] . . . because I was not superior enough to hold myself aloof—which is very queer and ridiculous of the simpler classes.

This is the first period: by my personal mode of existence I endeavoured to support the pseudonyms, the aesthetic work as a whole. Melancholy, incurably melancholy as I was, suffering prodigious griefs in my inmost soul, having broken in desperation from the world and all that is of the world, strictly brought up from my very childhood in the apprehension that the truth must suffer and be mocked and derided, spending a definite time every day in prayer and devout meditation, and being myself personally a penitent— in short, being what I was, I found (I do not deny it) a certain sort of satisfaction in this life, in this inverse deception, a satisfaction in observing that the deception succeeded so extraordinarily, that the public and I were on the most confidential terms, that I was quite in the fashion as the preacher of a gospel of worldliness, that though I was not in possession of the sort of distinction which can only be earned by an entirely different mode of life, yet in secret (and hence the more heartily loved) I was the darling of the public, regarded by every one as prodigiously interesting and witty. This satisfaction, which was my secret and which sometimes put me into an ecstasy, might have been a dangerous temptation. Not as though the world and such things could tempt me with their flattery and adulation. No, on that side I was safe. If I was to have been capsized, it would have to have been by this thought raised to a higher power, an obsession almost of ecstasy at the thought of how the deception was succeeding. This was an indescribable alleviation to a sense of resentment which smouldered in me from my childhood; because, long before I had seen it with my own eyes, I had been taught that falsehood, pettiness, and injustice ruled the world.—I often had to think of these words in *Either/Or*: 'If ye but knew what it is ye laugh at'—if ye but knew with whom ye have to do, who this *flâneur* is!

B. THE PERSONAL MODE OF EXISTENCE IN RELATION TO THE RELIGIOUS WORKS

In the month of December 1845 the manuscript of the *Concluding Postscript* was completely finished, and, as my custom was, I had delivered the whole of it at once to Luno [the printer]—which the suspicious do not have to believe on my word, since Luno's account-book is there to prove it. This work constitutes the turning-point in my whole activity as an author, inasmuch as it presents the 'problem', how to become a Christian. With this began the transition to the series of purely religious writings.

I perceived at once that my personal mode of existence must be remodelled to correspond with this change, or that I must try to give my contemporaries a different notion of my personal mode of existence. So I myself had already become aware of what must be done, when there occurred in the most opportune way a little incident in which I perceived a hint of Providence to help me to act decisively in that direction.

However, I cannot proceed farther with this subject until I have recalled to the reader's recollection the situation in Copenhagen at that juncture[B]—by a description which perhaps now will stand out in sharper relief by contrast with the present warlike situation. At that time there developed little by little the rather remarkable phenomenon that the entire population of Copenhagen became ironical—and just so much the more ironical in proportion as the people were more ignorant and uneducated. It was irony here and irony there, from one end to the other. If the case were not so serious, and if I could venture to contemplate it with a purely aesthetic interest, I do not deny that it is the most ludicrous thing I have ever beheld, and I really believe that one might travel far and still be lucky to encounter anything so fundamentally comical. The entire population of a city, with all the unemployed on the streets and alleys well in the lead, down to school-urchins and apprentices; all the legions of those classes which in our day are the only really privileged classes, those, namely, who amount to nothing, they become . . . (what they become) *en masse*; the entire population of a city, guilds, corporations, business men, persons of rank, they become (very much like a bourgeois sauntering out to the 'Deer Park'), they become . . . *en famille*; these thousands and thousands become . . . just about the one thing I would venture to assert it is impossible for them to become (especially *en masse* and *en famille*) they become *ironical*, by the help of a sheet, which in turn (ironically enough) leads the fashion by the help of editorial blackguards, and the fashion it sets is . . . irony. It is impossible, I believe, to think of anything more ludicrous. For irony implies a specific intellectual culture, such as is very rare in any generation —and this *cohue* and rabble were adepts in irony. Irony is absolutely unsocial; an irony which is in the majority is *eo ipso* not irony. Nothing is more certain than this, for it is implied in the very concept. Irony tends essentially towards one person as its limit, as is so justly stated in the Aristotelian saying,[13] that the ironical man does all 'for his own sake' (ἕαυτον ἕνεκα) —and here was an immense public, arm in arm, *in bona caritate*, become as ironical as the devil. But the case was too serious. This irony was of course sheer vulgarity. For even if the real instigator[14] possessed a talent by no means insignificant, it could not but become vulgarity in passing over to these thousands and thousands; and unfortunately vulgarity is always popular. So there was a demoralization which only too dreadfully recalls the punishment with which the Prophet of old in the name of the Lord threatened the Jews as the worst of all punishments, 'Children shall rule over you' [Isa. iii. 4]. It was a demoralization which, considering the proportions of the little land, actually threatened it with complete moral disintegration. To form a conception of the danger one must see at close range how even good-natured and worthy people, so soon as they become a 'crowd', turn into quite different beings. One must see at close range the want of character exhibited by otherwise upright people, who say, It is a shame, it is shocking for any one to do or to utter anything of the sort—and then they themselves contribute their little share to envelop the city in a snow-flurry of chatter and town-gossip. One must witness the hardness of heart which otherwise kindly people display in their capacity as 'the public', thinking that their inter-vention or non-intervention is a trifling thing—a trifling thing indeed which by the contributions of the many becomes a monster. One must see how laughter is feared above all other sorts of attack, how even a man who had boldly encountered mortal peril for a cause that did not concern him, would hardly hesitate to betray father and mother in case the danger were laughter. For an attack of this sort isolates a man as no other does, and at no point does it offer him the support of pathos, while frivolity and curiosity and sensuality grin, and the nervous cowardice which itself shuns such an attack incessantly cries, 'It is nothing', and the contemptible cowardice which buys itself off from attack by bribery or by currying favour with the person concerned, it too says, 'It is nothing', and even sympathy says, 'It is nothing'. It is terrible when in a little land chattering and grinning become a menace on becoming 'public opinion'. Denmark was on the point of being absorbed in Copenhagen, and Copenhagen was just in the act of becoming a mere provincial town. It is only too easy to bring this about, especially with the help of the press; and when this is accomplished it will require perhaps a generation to live it down.

But enough of this. It was important for me to alter my personal mode of existence to correspond with the fact that I was making the transition to the statement of religious problems. I must have an existence-form corresponding with this sort of authorship. The time, as I have said, was the month of December, and it was desirable that everything should be in readiness by the time the *Concluding Postscript* would come out. So the step was taken within this month of December. With the knowledge I possessed of the situation I readily perceived that it was enough to address two words to that organ of irony, which in a sense (i.e. if I had not been the man I am) had rather adroitly venerated and immortalized me—that two words would be enough to reverse dialectically my whole existence-relationship, by getting all that interminable public of ironical adepts to take aim at me, so that I should become the target of the irony of all men. Alas for me, the Magister of Irony![15]

The command was issued,[16] and in order that it might not be exploited as a newly invented and highly piquant form of irony, a pretty strong dose of the ethical was added by my requisition that I be made an object of the gross abuse of the loathsome organ of loathsome irony. That hydra of innumerable ironical heads naturally thought that I was crazy. The individuals who saw deeper into the affair beheld, not without a shudder, the leap which I made, or (because they thought only of what in a worldly sense is understood by worldliness and did not bethink them of what in a godly sense is understood by it) they found it beneath my dignity to take notice of such a thing, whereas I should have counted it beneath my dignity to have lived as a contemporary of such a demoralization without having acted decisively, content with the cheap virtue of behaving like 'the others', that is to say, shirking as far as possible all action, while journalistic vileness on a scale so disproportionately great was doubtless bringing people to their graves, mortifying and embittering, perhaps not always the direct objects of the attack, yet at all events their wives and children, their relatives and closest

57

friends, penetrating defilingly into every place, even
into the privacy of school-life, even into the sanctuary
of the Church, spitting out lies, gossip, insolence, and
urchin-pranks—all in the service of pernicious passion and paltry greed of money . . . and for all this a
blackguard[17] was 'responsible'! That in the service of
my idea this course which I took was the right one
I understood perfectly, and I did not vacillate. The
consequences thereof, of which certainly no one at the
moment was envious, I now lay historic claim to as
my lawful property, the value of which in perspective
my mind easily discerns.

I had now reckoned out that dialectically the situation would be appropriate for recovering the use of
indirect communication. While I was occupied solely
with religious productions I could count upon the
negative support of these daily douches of vulgarity,
which would be cooling enough in its effect to ensure
that the religious communication would not be too
direct, or too directly create for me adherents. The
reader could not relate himself directly to me; for
now, instead of the incognito of the aesthetical, I had
erected the danger of laughter and grins, by which
most people are scared away. And he even who was
not scared by this would be upset by the next obstacle,
by the thought that I had voluntarily exposed myself
to all this, giving proof of a sort of lunacy. Ah, yes!
so did the contemporaries doubtless judge of the
Roman knight[18] who made the immortal leap to save
his country! Ah, yes! and again, ah yes! for it was
dialectically the precise expression for Christian self-
denial—and I, poor wretch, the Magister of Irony,

became the pitiable target for the laughter of a 'highly esteemed public'.

The costume was correct. Every religious author is *eo ipso* polemical; for the world is not so good that the religious man can assume that he has triumphed or is in the party of the majority. A victorious religious author who is *in the world* is *eo ipso* not a religious author. The essentially religious author is always polemical, and hence he suffers under or suffers from the opposition which corresponds to whatever in his age must be regarded as the specific evil. If it be kings and emperors, popes and bishops . . . and powers that constitute the Evil, the religious author must be recognizable by the fact that he is the object of their attack. If it is the crowd—and prating and the public—and the beastly grin which is the Evil, he must be recognizable by the fact that he is the object of that sort of attack and persecution. And the essentially religious author has but one fulcrum for his lever, namely, a miraculous syllogism. When any one asks him on what he bases the claim that he is right and that it is the truth he utters, his answer is: I prove it by the fact that I am persecuted; this is the truth, and I can prove it by the fact that I am derided. That is, he does not substantiate the truth or the righteousness of his cause by appealing to the honour, reputation, &c., which he enjoys, but he does quite the contrary; for the essentially religious man is always polemical. Every religious writer, or speaker, or teacher, who absents himself from danger and is not present where it is, and where the Evil has its stronghold, is a deceiver, and that will eventually become apparent. For every one who comes to the gates of death and its doors open for him has to lay aside from him all the pomp and grandeur and wealth and worldly reputation, and the stars of knightly orders and other tokens of honour—whether they were distributed by kings and emperors or by the crowd and the public—has to lay them all. aside as things which are entirely inappropriate and superfluous. Only one exception is made, and that is with reference to the man who in his lifetime has been a religious writer or teacher or speaker. If he is found in possession of any such things, he is not allowed to lay them aside. No, they are packed up in a bundle and returned to him, and he is compelled to keep them and carry them, as a thief may be compelled to carry his stolen goods. And with that bundle he must enter the place where he is to be judged. Having been a religious teacher, he will be judged by the true religious teachers, who all of them so long as they lived were mocked, persecuted, derided, scorned, and spat upon. Ah! how frightful it is for the natural man to stand here on earth and be derided, mocked, and spat upon! More frightful still to stand in eternity with this bundle under his arm, or attired in his . . . finery!

The costume was correct. In a grinning age, such as that was of which I speak (and, in my opinion at least, the 'war'[19] has in this respect been a fortunate thing for Denmark), the religious author must, for God's sake! see well to it that he be derided above all others. If it is from the crowd the Evil proceeds, the contemporary religious author must, for God's sake! see well to it that he become the object of its persecution, and that in this respect he be found in the front line. And the estimate I formed of the crowd, which at one time even the more perspicacious may perhaps have considered a little exaggerated, now, in 1848,[c] now, by the help of the wild gesticulations of a real emergency (which are more effective than the weak voice of an individual and are like the raging of the elements), *now* the objection might rather be that I did not put it strongly enough. And that category, 'the individual', which was regarded as an oddity, the invention of an odd person—which in fact it is, for was not he who in a sense was the inventor of it, namely Socrates, called in his day 'the oddest' (ἀτοπώτατος)?[20] —the credit for having brought that category to notice in its time I would not exchange for a kingdom. If the crowd is the Evil, if chaos is what threatens us, there is salvation only in one thing, in becoming a single individual, in the thought of 'that individual' as an essential category. One triumph I have experienced, and one only, but that satisfies me absolutely, so that as a thinker I demand nothing more in this world. The revolutionary world-historical events of the past few months brought forward unripe, visionary men as the bewildered spokesmen of bewildering thoughts, and brought on the other hand to silence all that had hitherto in divers ways presumed to guide opinion— brought it either to silence or to the embarrassment of having to manufacture for itself in the greatest haste an entirely new dress. Every system was shattered— shattered as completely in the course of a few months as if between the present and the immediate past a whole generation had intervened. During this cata-

strophe I sat and read the proofs of a book (*Christian Discourses*) which, consequently, was written before
it. Not one single word was added or subtracted; it
expressed the view which I, 'the odd thinker', had
already for several years been propounding. One who
reads it will get the impression that the book was
written after the catastrophe. Such a world-historical
catastrophe, which ranks so high that not even the dissolution of the ancient world was so imposing, constitutes for every one who *then* was an author the absolute
tentamen rigorosum. I experienced the triumph of not
needing to modify or alter one tittle of what I had
written, the triumph, indeed, of seeing that what I had
written before the event will be, if any one now reads
it, far, far more intelligible than when it was written.
And now only one thing more. When some day my
lover comes, he will easily perceive that at the time I
was regarded as ironical the irony was by no means to
be found where 'the highly esteemed public' thought.
It was to be found—and this goes without saying, for
my lover cannot possibly be so foolish as to assume
that a public can understand irony, which is just as
impossible as to be an individual *en masse*—he will
perceive that the irony lay precisely in the fact that
within this aesthetic author, under this worldly appearance, was concealed the religious author, who just
at that time was consuming quite as much religiousness as commonly suffices for the provision of an entire
household. Moreover, my lover will perceive that
irony appeared again in relation to the next period,
and is to be discovered precisely in the fact which 'the
highly esteemed public' regarded as lunacy. In an

ironical generation (that great aggregation of fools) there remains nothing else for the ironical man to do but to invert the relationship and himself become the target for the irony of all men. My lover will perceive how it all fitted to a nicety, how my existence-relationship was transformed in precise correspondence with the requirement of my productivity. If I had not had an eye for this or courage enough for it, if I had altered the productivity but not the existence-relationship, the situation would have been undialectic and confused.

CHAPTER III

THE SHARE DIVINE GOVERNANCE*
HAD IN MY AUTHORSHIP

WHAT I have written up to this point has in a
sense been neither agreeable nor pleasant to
write. There is something painful in being obliged
to talk so much about oneself. Would to God I might
have ventured to hold my peace even longer than I
have, yea, even to die in silence about a subject which,
like my labour and my literary work, has occupied me
day and night. But now, thank God, now I breathe
freely, now I actually feel an urge to speak, now I
have come to the theme which I find inconceivably
pleasant to think about and to talk about. This God-
relationship of mine is the 'happy love' in a life which
has been in many ways troubled and unhappy. And
although the story of this love affair (if I dare call it
such) has the essential marks of a true love story, in
the fact that only one can completely understand it,
and there is no absolute joy but in relating it to one

* [Here, as in my book on *Kierkegaard*, I translate the
word *Styrelse* by 'Governance', hoping that this word may
serve to distinguish the providence which *rules* from the
providence which *provides* (which in Danish is denominated
by a different word), and that it may direct attention to the
fact that S. K. has in mind a divinity which shapes our ends
from *without*, by the providential ordering of events, not by
a mystical 'guidance' from *within*. I persist, with some
diffidence, in using this word, in spite of the fact that at
least one of the translators with whom I should like to be
in agreement is unwilling to adopt it.]

only, namely, the beloved, who in this instance is the Person by whom one is loved,* yet there is a joy also in talking about it to others.

* Perhaps now the reader may be ready to recognize how it is that what has been the misfortune, humanly speaking, of the whole productivity, what has more and more caused it to stand apart as a superfluity, instead of actually coming to grips with the situation, is the fact that it is too religious, or that the author's existence is too religious, that the author *qua* author has been absolutely weak, and therefore has been absolutely in need of God. If the author had been less weak, that is to say, in a human sense stronger (that is, less religious), he would as a matter of course have laid claim to the authorship as his own, he would presumably have acquired a number of confidants and friends, he would have made known beforehand to others what he proposed, would have taken counsel with them and asked their assistance; and they in turn, acting as godfathers, would have enlisted others, so that the authorship would have been interrelated with the instant and effective in the instant—instead of being a superfluity . . . such as God himself is in sooth, more than everything else and everybody else.—Perhaps now the reader may be ready to recognize why I have laboured with so much effort and sacrifice, day in and day out, to prevent falsehood from emerging, a falsehood, it is true, which (as it always does) would have brought me money, honour, reputation, applause, &c., the falsehood that what I had to deliver was 'what the age demands', that it is presented to the indulgent judgement of 'a highly respected public', *item* that it owes its success to the support and acclamation of this same highly respected public. In exact opposition to this, in the fear and love of God, I had to watch sleeplessly to ensure that the truth be expressed: that it was God's aid alone I relied on, that I owed nothing either to the public or to the age, except the wrong it has done me. I had to be on the watch to ensure that the truth might be expressed by the rousing epigram upon this age that at a time when everything was general assemblies and societies and committees, their appointment, continuation, and dissolution, whereas all the while nothing was done, that at this time there was bestowed upon a weakly and solitary

65

As for the fact that I have needed God's love, and how constantly I have needed it, day after day, year after year—to recall this to my mind and to report it exactly, I do not need the aid of memory or recollection, or of journals or diaries, nor do I need to check the one by the other, so vividly, so feelingly do I live it over again in this very instant. What could not this pen produce if it were a question of hardihood, of enthusiasm, of fervour to the verge of madness! And now that I am to talk about my God-relationship, about what every day is repeated in my prayer of thanksgiving for the indescribable things He has done for me, so infinitely much more than ever I could have expected, about the experience which has taught me to be amazed, amazed at God, at His love and at what a man's impotence is capable of with His aid, about what has taught me to long for eternity and not to

man the talent to work on a scale so great that any one might suppose it was more than the labour of a committee. In short, it was my duty to give expression, both in my personal existence and in my author-existence, to the fact that I every day ascertained and convinced myself anew that a God exists.—Perhaps now the reader may be ready to recognize why it was I found myself compelled to counteract in a finite sense my own effort, for the sake of ensuring that the responsibility should be all my own. I must in any case be quite alone, absolutely alone, yes, I must even reject assistance, lest my responsibility be too light. Given but one friend and one fellow worker, responsibility becomes a fraction—not to speak of getting a whole generation to come to one's aid. But in the service of truth the point for me was that if I were to go astray, if I were to become presumptuous, if what I said was untrue, Governance might have an absolutely sure hold on me, and that in the possibility of this examination which every instant hung over me I might be kept alert, attentive, obedient.

fear that I might find it tiresome, since it is exactly
the situation I need so as to have nothing else to do
but to give thanks. Now that I am to talk about this
there awakens in my soul a poetic impatience. More
resolutely than that king[21] who cried, 'My kingdom
for a horse', and blessedly resolute as he was not, I
would give all, and along with that my life, to be
able to find what thought has more blessedness in
finding than a lover in finding the beloved—to find
the 'expression', and then to die with this expression
on my lips. And lo! it presents itself—thoughts as
enchanting as the fruits in the garden of a fairy-tale,
so rich and warm and heartfelt; expressions so sooth-
ing to the urge of gratitude within me, so cooling to
my hot longing—it seems to me as if, had I a winged
pen, yes, ten of them, I still could not follow fast
enough to keep pace with the wealth which presents
itself. But no sooner have I taken pen in hand, at that
very instant I am incapable of moving it, as we say of
one that he cannot move hand or foot. In that situation not a line concerning this relationship gets put
down on paper. It seems to me as if I heard a voice
saying to me: Silly fellow, what does he imagine?
Does he not know that obedience is dearer to God
than the fat of rams?[22] Then I become perfectly quiet,
then there is time enough to write each letter with my
slow pen almost painfully. And if that poetic impatience awakes in me again for an instant, it seems as
though I heard a voice speaking to me as a teacher
speaks to a boy when he says: Now hold the pen right,
and form each letter with equal precision. And then I
can do it, then I dare not do otherwise, then I write

every word, every line, almost without knowing what the next word or the next line is to be. And afterwards when I read it over it satisfies me in quite a different way. For though it may be that one or another glowing expression escapes me, yet the production is quite a different one: it is the outcome, not of the poet's or the thinker's passion, but of godly fear, and for me it is a divine worship.

But what now at this instant I am living over again, or just now have been, is something I have experienced time and again during my whole activity as an author. It is said of the 'poet' that he invokes the muse to supply him with thoughts. This indeed has never been my case, my individuality prohibits me even from understanding it; but on the contrary I have needed God every day to shield me from too great a wealth of thoughts. Give a person such a productive talent, and along with that such feeble health, and verily he will learn to pray. I have been able at any instant to perform this prodigy, and I can do it still: I could sit down and continue to write for a day and a night, and again for a day and a night; for there was wealth sufficient for it. If I had done it, I should have been broken. Oh, even the least dietetic indiscretion, and I am in mortal danger. When I learn obedience, as I have described above, when I do the work as if it were a sternly prescribed task, hold the pen as I ought, write each letter with pains, then I can do it. And thus, many and many a time, I have had more joy in the relation of obedience to God than in thoughts that I produced. This, it can readily be perceived, is the expression of the fact that I can lay no claim to an immediate relationship with God, that I cannot and dare not say that it is He who immediately inserts the thoughts in me, but that my relationship to God is a reflection-relationship, is inwardness in reflection, as in general the distinguishing trait of my individuality is reflection, so that even in prayer my *forte* is thanksgiving.

Thus it is that in the course of my whole activity as an author I have constantly needed God's aid so as to be able to do the work simply as a prescribed task to which definite hours every day were allotted, outside of which it was not permissible to work. And if only once that rule was transgressed, I had to pay for it dearly. Nothing is less like my procedure than the stormy entrance of genius upon the scene, and then its tumultuous *finale*. Substantially I have lived like a clerk in his *comptoir*. From the very beginning I have been as it were under arrest and every instant have sensed the fact that it was not I that played the part of master, but that another was Master. I have sensed that fact with fear and trembling when He let me feel His omnipotence and my nothingness; have sensed it with indescribable bliss when I turned to Him and did my work in unconditional obedience. The dialectical factor in this is that whatever extraordinary gift may have been entrusted to me, it was entrusted as a precautionary measure with such elasticity that, if I were not to obey, it would strike me dead. It is as if a father were to say to his child: You are allowed to take the whole thing, it is yours; but if you will not be obedient and use it as I wish—very well, I shall not punish you by taking it from you; no, take it as yours

. . . it will smash you. Without God I am too strong for myself, and perhaps in the most agonizing of all ways am broken. Since I became an author I have never for a single day had the experience I hear others complain of, namely, a lack of thoughts or their failure to present themselves. If that were to happen to me, it would rather be an occasion for joy, that finally I had obtained a day that was really free. But many a time I have had the experience of being over-whelmed with riches, and every instant I bethought me with horror of the frightful torture of starving in the midst of abundance—if I do not instantly learn obedience, allow God to help me, and produce in the same fashion, as quietly and placidly as one performs a prescribed task.

But in still another sense I have needed God's aid, time and again, day after day, year after year, in the whole course of my activity as a writer. For He has been my one confidant, and only in reliance upon His cognizance have I dared to venture what I have ven-tured, and to endure what I have endured, and have found bliss in the experience of being literally alone in the whole vast world, alone because wherever I was, whether in the presence of all, or in the presence of a familiar friend, I was always clad in the costume of my deceit, so that I was then as much alone as in the darkness of the night; alone, not in the forests of America with their terrors and their perils, but alone in the company of the most terrible *possibilities*, which transform even the most frightful *actuality* into a refreshment and relief; alone, almost with human speech against me; alone with torments which have taught me more than one new annotation to the text about the thorn in the flesh;[23] alone with decisions in which one had need of the support of friends, the whole race if possible; alone in dialectical tensions which (without God) would drive any man with my imagination to madness; alone in anguish unto death; alone in the face of the meaninglessness of existence, without being able, even if I would, to make myself intelligible to a single soul—but what am I saying, 'to a single soul'?—nay, there were times when it could not be said in the common phrase, '*that* alone was lacking', times when I could not make myself intelligible to myself. When now I reflect that years were passed in this manner, I shudder. When but for a single instant I see amiss, I sink in deep waters. But when I see aright and find repose in the assurance of God's cognizance, blessedness returns again.

And now for details. It would be in vain for me to attempt to relate how I have sensed God's present aid. As in the inexplicable occurrence which often was repeated, that when I did something without knowing why or even thinking to ask why, when as a simple person I followed the prompting of my natural inclination, that then this which for me had a purely personal significance verging on the accidental, that this then proved to have an entirely different and a purely ideal significance when it was viewed later in relation to the authorship as a whole; that, strangely enough, much I had done personally was exactly what I should have done *qua* author. It has been inexplicable to me that trivial and, as it seemed, accidental circumstances in my life (which, it must be said, were made to loom large by my imagination) brought me into a definite situation where I did not understand myself and became melancholy—and, lo! there developed from this a mood, and precisely the mood I had use for in relation to the work I was then occupied with, and precisely at the right place. For the productivity has never suffered the least check; what was needed for use was always at hand, just at the instant it was needed. The whole productivity has had in a certain sense an uninterruptedly even course, as if I had had nothing else to do but to copy daily a definite portion of a printed book.

However, in this accounting I must make a more precise reckoning of the share Governance had in the authorship. For in case I were to affirm out and out that from the very first instant I had a survey of the whole authorship, or that at every moment, stage by stage, I had by anticipation so far exhausted the possibilities that later reflection had not taught me anything, not even this other thing, that though what I had done was surely right, yet only afterwards was I in a position to understand thoroughly that this was so—if I were to do this, it would be a denial of God and dishonesty towards Him. No, I must say truly that I cannot understand the whole, just because to the merest insignificant detail I understand the whole, but what I cannot understand is that now I can understand it and yet cannot by any means say that at the instant of commencing it I understood it so precisely —though it is I that have carried it out and made every step with reflection. In the parlance of pure bosh one could easily explain this by saying, as some one has said of me, without having any conception of my literary work as a totality, that I had a genius for reflection. But just because I acknowledge the justice of ascribing to me reflection—I am verily too reflective not to perceive that this juxtaposition of reflection and genius explains nothing. For just so far forth as one has genius, he has not reflection, and vice versa, inasmuch as reflection is precisely the negation of immediacy.

Were I now to express with the utmost categorical precision the share Governance had in my whole activity as a writer, I know no more suggestive or decisive expression than this: it is Governance that has educated me, and the education is reflected in the process of the productivity. In view of this it must be admitted that what I set forth above about the whole aesthetic production being a deceit is not quite true, for this expression assumes a little too much in the way of consciousness. At the same time, however, it is not altogether false, for I have been conscious of being under instruction, and that from the very first. The process is this: a poetic and philosophic nature is put aside in order to become a Christian. But the unusual feature is that the two movements begin simultaneously, and hence this is a conscious process, one is able to perceive how it comes about, the second movement does not supervene after a series of years which separate it from the first. So the aesthetic production is certainly a deceit, yet in another sense it is a necessary elimination. The religious is present from the very first instant and has a decisive predominance, but for a while it waits patiently to give the poet leave to talk himself out, yet all the time on the watch with Argus eyes to make sure the poet does not fool it.*

It is from this point of view, I take it, that the significance my authorship has for this age is to be seen to most advantage. If with one word I were to express my judgement of this age, I would say that it lacks religious education (understanding this word in the broadest and deepest sense). The thing of becoming and of being a Christian is now a triviality. The aesthetical has plainly got the upper hand. By 'going farther' than the mere thing of being a Christian (which every one is as a matter of course) one has got back again to or into a refined aesthetic and intellectual paganism with the admixture of a dash of Christianity. The task which has to be proposed to the majority of people in Christendom is: Away from the 'poet'! or away from having a relation to or from having one's life in that which the poet declaims; Away from speculation! from the fantastic conceit (which is at the same time an impossibility) of having one's life in that (instead of existing)—and to become a Christian! The first movement (away from the

* This thought, that it is the 'poet' that must be got rid of, already finds its expression in *Either/Or*, although when it is understood in view of the authorship as a totality this thing of getting away from or back from the 'poet' has naturally a deeper meaning than the Second part of *Either/Or* could explain. That this is the case with *Either/Or* was already noted in the *Concluding Postscript*, p. 188, l. 21 seq. (S. K. vii, p. 238 f.). Indeed the transition made in *Either/Or* is substantially that from a poet-existence to an ethical existence.

poetical) constitutes the total significance of the aesthetic production within the totality of the authorship. The second movement (away from speculation) is that of the *Concluding Postscript*, which, while it draws or edits the whole aesthetic production to its own advantage by way of illuminating its problem, which is the problem of 'becoming a Christian', makes the same movement in another sphere: Away from speculation! from the System, &c.—to become a Christian. The movement is, **Back!** And although it is all done without 'authority',[24] there is, nevertheless, something in the accent which recalls a policeman when he faces a riot and says, Back! Hence also more than one of the pseudonyms applies this expression to himself, saying that he is a policeman, a member of the detective force.

And now as for me, the author, what, according to my opinion, is my relation to the age? Am I perhaps the 'Apostle'?[25] Abominable! I have never given an occasion for such a judgement. I am a poor insignificant person. Am I then the teacher, the educator? No, not that at all; I am he who himself has been educated, or whose authorship expresses what it is to be educated to the point of becoming a Christian. In the fact that education is pressed upon me, and in the measure that it is pressed, I press in turn upon this age; but I am not a teacher, only a fellow student.

To illuminate farther the share of Governance in the authorship, it is necessary to explain, so far as I have an explanation at my disposal, how it was I became an author.

About my *vita ante acta* (i.e. from childhood until I became an author) I cannot expatiate here at any length, however remarkable, as it seems to me, was the way I was predisposed from my earliest childhood, and step by step through the whole development, to become exactly the sort of author I became. For the sake of what follows I must allude, however, to a few traits of my earlier life, which I do with the diffidence a person surely must always feel when he has to speak quite personally about himself.

From a child I was under the sway of a prodigious melancholy, the depth of which finds its only adequate measure in the equally prodigious dexterity I possessed of hiding it under an apparent gaiety and *joie de vivre*. So far back as I can barely remember, my one joy was that nobody could discover how unhappy I felt. This proportion (the equally great magnitude of melancholy and of the art of dissimulation) signifies that I was relegated to myself and to a relationship with God. As a child I was sternly and seriously brought up in Christianity. Humanly speaking, it was a crazy upbringing. Already in my earliest childhood I broke down under the grave impression which the melancholy old man who laid it upon me himself sank under. A child—what a crazy thing!—travestied as an old man! Frightful! What wonder then that there were times when Christianity appeared to me the most inhuman cruelty—although never, even when I was farthest from it, did I cease to revere it, with a firm determination that (especially if I did not myself make the choice of becoming a Christian) I would never initiate any one into the difficulties which I knew and

which, so far as I have read and heard, no one else has
alluded to. But I have never definitely broken with
Christianity nor renounced it. To attack it has never
been my thought. No, from the time when there
could be any question of the employment of my
powers, I was firmly determined to employ them all to
defend Christianity, or in any case to present it in its
true form. For very early indeed, by the help of my
upbringing, I was in a position to ascertain for myself
how seldom Christianity is presented in its true form,
how they who defend it most commonly betray it, and
how seldom its opponents really hit the mark—although, in my opinion at least, they often squarely hit
established Christendom, which might rather be called
the caricature of true Christianity, or a monstrous
amount of misunderstanding, illusion, &c., mixed
with a sparing little dose of true Christianity. So I
loved Christianity in a way: to me it was venerable—
it had, to be sure, humanly speaking, rendered me
exceedingly unhappy. This corresponds to my relationship with my father, the person whom I loved most
deeply. And what is the meaning of this? The point
precisely is that he made me unhappy—but out of
love. His error did not consist in lack of love, but in
mistaking a child for an old man. To love him who
makes one happy, is to a reflective mind an inadequate
definition of what love is; to love him who made one
unhappy out of malice, is virtue; but to love him who
out of love, though by a misunderstanding, yet out of
love, made one unhappy—that is the formula never yet
enunciated, so far as I know, but nevertheless the
normal formula in reflection for what it is to love.

So I went forth into life, favoured in every way, so far as intellectual gifts go and outward circumstances. Everything was done and continued to be done to develop my mind as richly as possible. Self-confident —yet with a decided sympathy or predilection for suffering, or for whatever in any way is suffering or oppressed. In a certain sense I may say that I went out into life with a proud and almost foolhardy bearing. I have never at any instant in my life been deserted by the faith that one can do what one will— only one thing excepted, all else unconditionally, but one thing not, the throwing off of the melancholy in whose power I was. What I am saying will seem to others a vain conceit, but so it was with me in truth, as truly as what I tell next, which to others again will seem a conceit. I say that it never remotely occurred to me that in my generation there lived or was to be born a man who had the upper hand of me—and in my inmost self I was the most wretched of all men. It never remotely occurred to me that, even if I were to attempt the most foolhardy enterprise, I should not be victorious—only one thing excepted, all else absolutely, but one thing not, the throwing off of the melancholy from which and from its attendant suffering I was never entirely free even for a day. This, however, must be understood in connexion with the fact that I was very early initiated into the thought that to conquer means to conquer in an infinite sense, which in a finite sense means to suffer. So this corresponded with my melancholy's inward apprehension that, in a finite sense, I was utterly good for nothing. What reconciled me with my fate and with my sufferings was that I, the so unhappy, so much tortured prisoner, had obtained this unlimited freedom of being able to deceive, so that I was allowed to be absolutely alone with my pain. It goes without saying that this was quite enough to render all my other abilities anything but merry for me. When this is given (i.e. such a pain and such a close reserve), it depends upon the personal characteristics of the individual whether this lonesome inward torment finds its expression and satisfaction in hating men and cursing God, or in the very reverse. The latter was my situation. As far back as I can remember I was in agreement with myself about one thing, that for me there was no comfort or help to be looked for in others. Sated with the many other things bestowed upon me, filled as a man with longing after death, as a spirit desirous of the longest possible life, my thought was, as the expression of a melancholy love for men, to be helpful to them, to find comfort for them, above all clearness of thinking, and that especially about Christianity. The thought goes very far back in my recollection that in every generation there are two or three who are sacrificed for the others, are led by frightful sufferings to discover what redounds to the good of others. So it was that in my melancholy I understood myself as singled out for such a fate.

So I fared forth into life—initiated into all possible enjoyments, yet never really enjoying, but rather (to indulge the one pleasure I had in connexion with the pain of melancholy) labouring to produce the impression that I enjoyed. I fared forth into acquaintance with all sorts of men, yet it never occurred to me that

I had a confidant in any of them, and certainly it never occurred to any one of them that he was my confidant. That is to say, I was constrained to be and was an observer. By such a life, as an observer and as spirit, I was extraordinarily enriched by experiences, got to see quite near at hand that aggregation of pleasures, passions, dispositions, feelings, &c., got practice in seeing a man through and through and also in imitating him. My imagination and my dialectic constantly had material enough to operate with, and time enough, free from all bustle, to be idle. For long periods I have been employed with nothing else but the performance of dialectical exercises with an adjunct of imagination, trying out my mind as one tunes an instrument—but I was not really living. I was tossed about in life, tempted by many and the most various things, unfortunately also by errors, and, alas! also by the path of perdition. So I was in my twenty-fifth year, to myself an enigmatically developed and extraordinary possibility, the significance of which and its character I did not understand, in spite of the most eminent reflection which if possible understood everything. I understood one thing, that my life would be most properly employed in doing penance; but in the proper sense of the word I had not lived, except in the character of spirit; a man I had never been, and child or youth even less.

Then my father died. The powerful religious impressions of my childhood acquired a renewed power over me, now softened by reflection. Also I had now become so much older that I fitted better to my upbringing, which has just this misfortune, that it does not turn out completely to my advantage until I am forty years old. For my misfortune (almost I might say from my birth, completed by my upbringing) was . . . not to be a man. But when one is a child—and the other children play or jest or whatever else they do; ah! and when one is a youth—and the other young people make love and dance or whatever else they do—and then, in spite of the fact that one is a child or a youth, then to be a spirit! Frightful torture! Even more frightful if one by the help of imagination knows how to perform the trick of appearing to be the youngest of all. But this misfortune is already diminished when one is forty years old, and in eternity it does not exist. I have never had any immediacy, and therefore, in the ordinary human sense of the word, I have never lived. I began at once with reflection; it is not as though in later years I had amassed a little reflection, but I am reflection from first to last. In the two ages of immediacy (childhood and youth) I, with the dexterity reflection always possesses, helped myself out, as I was compelled to do, by some sort of counterfeit, and not being quite clear myself about the talents bestowed upon me, I suffered the pain of not being like the others—which naturally at that period I would have given everything to be able to be, if only for a short time. A spirit can very well put up with not being like the others—indeed that is precisely the negative definition of spirit. But childhood and youth stand in a close relation to the generic qualification expressed in the species, the race; and just for this reason it is the greatest torment of that period not to be like the others, or, as in my case, so strangely topsy-turvy as to begin at that point where a few in every generation end, whereas the majority, who live merely in the factors of the soulish-bodily synthesis, never reach it—that is to say, the qualification spirit. But for this same reason I have my life now before me, in a sense very different from the ordinary meaning of that phrase. Nothing is more completely unknown and foreign to me than that wistful longing for childhood and youth. I thank my God that all this is through with, and I feel happier with every day I grow older—yet only blessed in the thought of eternity, for the temporal never is and never will be the element of spirit, but in a sense it must mean suffering for it.

An observer will perceive how everything was set in motion and how dialectically: I had a thorn in the flesh, intellectual gifts (especially imagination and dialectic) and culture in superabundance, an enormous development as an observer, a Christian upbringing that was certainly very unusual, a dialectical relationship to Christianity which was peculiarly my own, and in addition to this I had from childhood a training in obedience, obedience absolute, and I was armed with an almost foolhardy faith that I was able to do anything, only one thing excepted, to be a free bird, though but for one whole day, or to slip out of the fetters of melancholy in which another power held me bound. Finally, in my own eyes I was a penitent. The impression this now makes upon me is as if there were a Power which from the first instant had been observant of this and said, as a fisherman says of a fish, Let it run awhile, it is not yet the moment to pull it in. And strangely enough there is something that reaches far

back in my recollection, impossible as it is for me to
say when I began this practice or why such a thing
ever occurred to me: I prayed to God regularly, i.e.
every day, that He would give me zeal and patience to
perform the work He would assign me.

Thus I became an author.

Before my real activity as an author began there was
an occurrence, or rather a fact (*factum*^A—to use a word
which etymologically implies that I had an active part
to play), since presumably an occurrence would not
have been sufficient, for I had to be the active agent in
the affair. I cannot elucidate this *factum* more particularly, telling in what it consisted, how terribly dialectical it was in its combination (although in another
sense it was quite simple), or what really constituted
the collision. I can only beg the reader not to think of
revelations or anything of that sort, for with me everything is dialectical. On the other hand, I shall describe
the consequence of this *factum* in so far as it serves to
illuminate the authorship. It was a duplex *factum*.
However much I had lived and experienced in another
sense, I had, in a human sense, leapt over the stages of
childhood and youth; and this lack, I suppose, must
(in the opinion of Governance) be somehow made up
for: instead of having been young, I became a poet,
which is a second youth. I became a poet; but with
my predisposition for religion, or rather, I may say,
with my decided religiousness, this *factum* was for me
at the same time a religious awakening,²⁶ so that I
came to understand myself in the most decisive sense
in the experience of religion, or in religiousness, to

which, however, I had already put myself into relation as a possibility. The *factum* made me a poet. Had I not been the man I was, and the occurrence, on the other hand, what it was, and if I had not taken the active part I did take, it would have amounted to nothing more: I should have become a poet, and then perhaps after the lapse of many years should have come into relation with the religious. But just because I was so religiously developed as I was, the *factum* took far deeper hold of me and, in a sense, nullified what I had become, namely, the poet. It nullified it, or at least I was led simultaneously to begin in the same moment at two points, yet in such a way that this thing of being a poet was essentially irrelevant to me, something I had become by means of another person —on the other hand the religious awakening, though it was certainly not a thing I had experienced by means of myself, yet it was in accordance with myself, that is to say, in this thing of becoming a poet I did not recognize myself in a deeper sense, but rather in the religious awakening.

Here the reader can easily perceive the explanation of all the difficulty of the authorship, but he must note that the author was at the same time conscious of this. What was to be done? Well, obviously the poetical had to be evacuated, anything else was impossible for me. But the whole aesthetic production was put under arrest by the religious. The religious agreed to this elimination but incessantly spurred it on, as though it were saying, Are you not now through with that?*

* One will now perhaps be aware of what I myself promptly understood as the misfortune, humanly speaking,

While the poetical works were being produced the
author was living under strict religious rules.*

of the whole authorship. It was too grandiose, it found no
appropriate place in any instant of reality, partly because
of the very great haste with which it was produced, and
partly because it comprehended such a decisive development as that from the aesthetical to the religious, the
Christian. In relation to *Either/Or* as the first work, this
misfortune was obscured; there was as yet no scale presented, nor was the duplicity posited. People regarded
Either/Or as the fruit of many years' labour. That illusion
helped, and there were many other factors which helped
Either/Or. For example, by the help of the illusion people
could perceive the pains that were taken in a stylistic sense;
and yet *Either/Or* was written in the shortest time, and
perhaps the least pains were taken about style. But this is
natural. The public could also perceive that the first part
of *Either/Or* was written several years before the second
part, and the reality is just the contrary: the second part
was written first. So it was with *Either/Or*. But when
subsequently the illusion was made impossible and the scale
was furnished, no one could come to any other conclusion
than that it was hasty work and not worth the trouble of
following. Naturally enough. The literary output upon
which I had spent five years would ordinarily have required
fifteen. Perhaps one will also understand now, and be in
agreement with me, that I did not want any reviews[27] because
I could not expect any essential review. How could I in
such a little land count upon any contemporary who had
the presuppositions and likewise the time to survey such a
consciously crafty production? And direct communication
I dared not use because I understood silence as my religious
duty. Or is it possible that it could really have occurred for
a single instant to any man when he got hold of *Either/Or*
that the author was a religious man, or that he himself, if he
were to follow my activity as an author, would in the course
of three or four years of such a journey find himself in the
midst of the most decisive Christian productivity?

* One will perceive the significance of the pseudonyms
and why I must be pseudonymous in relation to all aesthetic
productions, because I led my own life in entirely different

In a certain sense it was not at all my original intention to become a religious author. My intention was to evacuate as hastily as possible the poetical—and then go out to a country parish. By this compass I steered. I felt myself foreign to the whole poetical production, but I could do no other. It was not my original intention, as I have said, to become a religious *author*. I had reflected that the most vigorous expression of the fact that I had been a religious man and that the pseudonyms were something foreign to me was the abrupt transition—to go immediately out in the country to seek a cure as a country parson.

However, the urge of productivity in me was so great that I could not do otherwise; I let the *Two Edifying Discourses* come out, and I came to an understanding with Governance. There was allowed me again a period for poetical production, but always under the arrest of the religious, which was on the watch, as if it said, Will you not soon be through with that? And I found a way to satisfy the religious by becoming a religious author.

Governance had me now securely bound. Like a suspicious character perhaps, I have been put on a very spare diet. I have been accustomed so to live that the maximum time I expect to have left is a year—sometimes, and not seldom, when a special tension is required, I live with the prospect of a week, yes, even of a day. And Governance had put checks upon me in every sense. So far as the aesthetic production was

categories and understood from the beginning that this productivity was of an interim nature, a deceit, a necessary process of elimination.

concerned, I was unable to escape from Governance by way of leading my life in the aesthetical. For even if the religious had not been in the background, that thorn in the flesh would have prevented any such thing. And in relation to the religious production, Governance had a check on me in the fact that I did not arrogate anything to myself because I understood myself to be in too great a debt.

And now I come to an expression about myself which I am accustomed to use of myself when I talk to myself, an expression which is relative to the inverse procedure of the whole productivity (that I did not begin by saying whither I designed to go), and relative to me also in my capacity as observer, along with my consciousness of being one who himself is in need of upbringing. The expression I use is, that in relation to the intellectual and religious fields, and with a view to the concept of existence, and hence to the concept of Christianity, I am like a spy in a higher service, the service of the idea. I have nothing new to proclaim; I am without authority, being myself hidden in a deceit; I do not go to work straightforwardly but with indirect cunning; I am not a holy man; in short, I am a spy who in his spying, in learning to know all about questionable conduct and illusions and suspicious characters, all the while he is making inspection is himself under the closest inspection. Observe that this is the sort of people the police make use of. They will hardly select for their purposes the sort of people whose life was always highly honest; all that they take into account is that they are experienced, cunning, intriguing, shrewd people who can nose anything out, always follow a clue and bring things to light. Hence the police are far from disinclined to have under their thumb a person who by reason of his *vita ante acta* they can compel to put up with everything, to obey, and to make no fuss about his personal dignity. So, too, it is with Governance, only that there is this endless difference between it and the civil police, that Governance, being merciful love, employs such a person just for love's sake, saves him and educates him all the while he is employing his shrewdness, which is thus sanctified and consecrated. But such a person, as one who himself stands in need of betterment, understands that he is bound to the most unconditional obedience. It is certain that of every man God can require all, that man must put up with everything, but it is also certain that the consciousness of earlier errors helps considerably to encourage promptness and nimbleness in this respect.*

* If any one were to make what I should call the sharp-witted observation, 'Then if that is the case, if the notion that you are a spy is true, your whole activity as an author is a sort of misanthropic treachery, a crime against humanity'; then I should answer, 'Oh yes, the crime is that I have loved God in a *Christian* way.' I have not endeavoured with the slightest fraction of the talents granted me to express the thought (which perhaps is what is meant by loving men) that the world is good, that it loves the truth, or desires the good, that the human race is the truth or even is God, and that the task therefore (Goetheo-Hegelian) is to content the age. On the contrary, I have endeavoured to express the thought that the world, if not bad, is mediocre, that 'what the age demands' is foolishness and frippery, that in the eyes of the world the truth is a ludicrous exaggeration; and that the Good must suffer. I have endeavoured to express the thought that to employ the category 'race' to indicate what it is to be a man, and especially as an indication of the

But in any case this surely is evident, that with
respect to reflection and shrewdness Christendom has

highest attainment, is a misunderstanding and mere paganism, because the race, mankind, differs from an animal race
not merely by its general superiority as a race, but by the
human characteristic that every single individual within the
race (not merely distinguished individuals but every individual) is more than the race. This follows from the relation
of the individual to God, and essentially this is Christianity,
whose category, 'the individual', is so much derided by this
highly lauded Christian age. For to relate oneself to God
is a far higher thing than to be related to the race and
through the race to God. This is what I have endeavoured
to express. I have not declaimed or thundered, and I have
not lectured, but I have made it plain that this is the case
also in our age, that our age and generation is pitifully confused about the good and the true. I have endeavoured to
make this manifest by all the cunning and craftiness I had
at my command. In opposition to the theory and practice
of living which humanly and with human self-complacency
loves what it is to be a man and turns traitor to God—in
opposition to this I have committed the crime of loving God
and have endeavoured by every means (but indirectly, *qua*
spy) to make this treason manifest. Supposing that I had
been free to use my talents as I pleased (and that it was not
the case that another Power was able to compel me every
moment when I was not ready to yield to fair means), I
might from the first moment have converted my whole
productivity into the channel of the interests of the age, it
would have been in my power (if such betrayal were not
punished by reducing me to naught) to become what the
age demands, and so would have been (Goetheo-Hegelian)
one more testimony to the proposition that the world is good,
that the race is the truth and that this generation is the court
of last resort, that the public is the discoverer of the truth
and its judge, &c. For by this treason I should have attained
extraordinary success in this world, &c. Instead of this I
became (under compulsion) a spy. In this there is nothing
meritorious: I certainly do not build my salvation upon it.
Yet it delights me childishly that I have served in this way,
whereas in relation to God I offer this whole activity of mine

exceeded all limits. Immediate pathos is of no avail—
even if in immediate pathos one were to sacrifice his
life. The age has at its disposal too much reflection
and shrewdness not to be able to reduce his significance
to zero. Even for a martyr to accomplish anything in
these times he must possess reflection, in order to so
intrigue the age that it cleaves to him even when it puts
him to death—that thus the awakening may follow.

So it is I understand myself in my activity as an
author. It makes the illusion of Christendom evident
and opens the eyes to what it is to become a Christian.
Whether there exist such a high grade of religiousness
that in its eyes the whole aesthetic production cannot
be regarded as a necessary elimination, or as a deceit,
but is simply something that must be repented of, I do
not know. I have never understood it thus, and surely
such a thought will not occur to any one before I utter
it. But since with me everything is reflection, it is a
matter of course that this thought has not escaped my
notice. I can imagine this objection made from the
point of view of a scrupulous and pusillanimous notion
of the duty of telling the truth, a notion which consistently leads to being always mute for fear of saying
something false; and since silence may be a falsehood,
it consistently leads to the false dilemma: Do it or
don't do it; be silent or speak out; both are equally

with more diffidence than a child when it gives as a present
to the parents an object which the parents had presented to
the child. Oh, but the parents surely are not so cruel that,
instead of looking kindly upon the child and entering into its
notion that this is a present, they take the gift away from the
child and say, This is our property. So it is also with God: He
is not so cruel when one as a gift brings to Him ... His own.

futile. But timorousness to the verge of lunacy is hardly to be regarded as a higher form of religiousness. Teleological suspension in relation to the communication of truth (i.e. to suppress something for the time being in order that the truth may become truer) is a plain duty to the truth and is comprised in the responsibility a man has before God for a proper use of the reflection bestowed upon him.·

Well acquainted as I was with the suffering of inwardness in relation to the task of becoming a Christian, and strictly brought up as I was in this apprehension, the other side of the matter almost escaped me. Here Governance came to my help, and helped me in such wise that the consequence of what I did turned out truly to my advantage and to the advantage of my cause. If one may compare intellectual talents with a stringed instrument, I may say that not only was I not put out of tune, but I acquired an extra string to my instrument.[28] This was the fruit of the more complete experimental education in what it means to become a Christian. For at the decisive instant when I was radically altering my existence-relationship on account of the *Concluding Postscript*, I had opportunity to observe what one will never believe until he has experienced it, namely, this Christian truth that love is hated. Verily nothing has ever been farther from me than pretension to social superiority (*Fornemhed*). Being myself of humble origin, I have loved the common people, or what is spoken of as the simple classes. So indeed I did, as I well know, for in that I found a melancholy joy—and yet it was precisely they who were incited against me and made to believe that I gave myself airs of superiority. If I had really been superior (*fornem*), this would never have happened to me. Observe that here we have precisely the Christian proportions, and on a scale so great that it enabled me to illuminate Christianity from this side. The complaint which might have been brought against my mode of life (if the merely human were to be the judge, and not Christianity) can only be expressed thus: that I have not shown sufficient regard for my personal dignity, have not been 'superior'; that humanly speaking I have in a light-minded way (Christianly understood, a God-fearing way) made sport of worldly honour and prestige, that by impairing possibly my own worldly prestige I have at the same time contributed to impair worldly prestige in general. As I have said, I should regard it as perfectly natural if in consideration of this the people who are in the enjoyment of superior place and reputation had shown themselves a bit hostile, and hence I am the more grateful for the fact that exactly the opposite is and has been the case. But the fact that, because I have lived as I have, I am exposed to the hatred of the common people—that is to say, because I have not been 'superior' enough, I have therefore been attacked—that is lunacy . . . and the Christian proportion.

Thus it is that the whole literary activity turns upon the problem of becoming a Christian in Christendom; and this is the expression of the share Governance had in the authorship, that it is the author himself who has been educated, yet with consciousness of this from the very first.

EPILOGUE

'BUT what have you done now?' I hear some-body say. 'Do you not perceive what you have lost in the eyes of the world by making this explana-tion and public acknowledgement?' To be sure, I perceive it very clearly. I have lost thereby what in a Christian sense it is a loss to possess, namely, every worldly form of the interesting. I lose the interesting distinction of proclaiming the seductive craftiness of pleasure, the glad report of life's most subtle enjoy-ments, and the insolence of derision. I lose the interesting distinction of being an interesting pos-sibility, suggestive of the query whether it might not after all be the case that he who represented the ethical with warmth and enthusiasm—whether he might not after all be exactly the opposite, *either* in one way *or* another, since it is (so interestingly) im-possible to say which he is. I lose the interesting distinction of being an enigma, seeing it is impossible to know whether this thorough-going defence of Christianity is not a covert attack most cunningly conceived. This interesting distinction I lose, and for it is substituted, at the farthest remove from the interesting, the *direct communication* that the problem was, and is, how to become a Christian. The interest-ing is what I have lost in the eyes of the crowd, in the world's eyes—if indeed I get off so easily as to lose only that, and the world does not become enraged at the fact that a man has presumed to be so crafty.

True enough, things are going backward with me,

in a sense—though in a Christian sense it is forward. As an author I began with the tremendous advantage of being regarded privately as not much better than a scoundrel—but naturally all the more likeable on that account, especially as I was so interesting and witty. This was needed in order to get the 'crowd' of Christians a little bit on my side. Even if one were a saint, one could not begin with holiness without losing the game in advance. For in the age of reflection in which we live people are prompt to parry, and even the death of the saint is of no avail. No, in the sphere of reflection everything must be done inversely. Thus it was I began. At that time I stood at the pinnacle of favour with the human crowd, and (since we live in Christendom where all are Christians) with the Christian crowd also, all the novel-readers of both sexes, the aesthetically refined, the clever wits, all of whom are at the same time Christians.

This was the beginning. As time went on and I got farther ahead, and the great public became aware or had a suspicion (ah! this was going backward with a vengeance!), had a suspicion that I really was not so bad after all, the public fell away more and more, and I began to be included under the tiresome category of the good. And in the meanwhile, I of the edifying discourses, keeping pace with the aesthetic production, perceived with joy that 'that single individual whom I with joy and gladness call *my* reader' became more than one, became a rather larger figure, yet certainly not anything like a public. And then when I performed a decisive act[B] which had a little bit of

Christian flavour about it, an act which at the same time I was conscious of performing as a benefaction to little Denmark, and an act which will give me unconditional joy at my hour of death—that is to say, when I cast myself as a sacrifice before the insurrection of vulgarity—then I was regarded by the public as crazy and queer, condemned almost as a criminal. Naturally enough, for there was not the least trace of the scoundrel or the rascal in what I did. How perfectly this all fits together! I do not see how more could be required of a spy.

And now—now I am no longer interesting. That the problem of becoming a Christian, that this *really* should be the fundamental thought in my whole activity as an author—how tiresome! And this thing of *The Seducer's Diary*,* this tremendously witty production! Why, it seems now that even this belonged to the plan! If any one asks me in a purely aesthetic interest what my judgement is about the aesthetic production, I will not make any attempt

---

* Psychologically it is quite remarkable, and worthy perhaps to be recorded, that a person to whose name I will concede a place here in order to take him with me—that Herr P. L. Møller quite rightly regarded 'The Diary of the Seducer' as the central point in the whole authorship. That reminds me so vividly of the motto to *The Stages on Life's Road*—precisely the work which he, from the point of view of 'The Diary of the Seducer', fell foul of and foully fell over—which motto I therefore reminded him of in a little lesson[29] I gave him, but it may be appropriate to repeat it here since it is well adapted as an epigram to preserve a pious memory of Herr P. L. Møller's aesthetical and critical services on behalf of my authorship: 'Such works are mirrors: when an ape peers into them, no Apostle can be seen looking out.'

to conceal the fact that I know perfectly well what has been accomplished, but I will add that for me even the aesthetic value of the accomplishment consists in a deeper sense in the indication it furnishes of how momentous the decision to become a Christian is. In the sphere of immediacy it is a perfectly *straightforward* thing to become a Christian; but the truth and inwardness of the reflective expression for becoming a Christian is measured by the value of the thing which reflection is bound to reject. For one does not become a Christian by means of reflection, but to become a Christian in reflection means that there is another thing to be rejected; one does not reflect oneself into being a Christian, but out of another thing in order to become a Christian; and this is more especially the case in Christendom, where one must reflect oneself out of the semblance of being a Christian. The nature of the other thing decides how deep, how significant, the movement of reflection is. What precisely characterizes the nature of the reflection is the fact that from a distance, and from how great a distance, one reaches the point of becoming a Christian. The reflection is defined by the difficulty, which is greater just in proportion to the value of the thing left behind.

Thus it is, as I believe, that I have rendered a service to the cause of Christianity while I myself have been educated by the process. He who was regarded with astonishment as about the shrewdest fellow (and this was attained with *Either/Or*), he to whom the place of 'the interesting man' was willingly conceded (and this was attained with *Either/Or*)—

precisely he, as it turned out, was engaged in the service of Christianity, had consecrated* himself to this from the very instant he began that pseudonymous activity, he, personally and as an author, was striving to bring out this simple thing about becoming a Christian. The movement is not from the simple to the interesting, but from the interesting to the simple, the thing of becoming a Christian, which is the place where the *Concluding Postscript* comes in, the 'turning-point', as I have called it, of the whole authorship, which states the 'Problem' and at the same time, by indirect attack and Socratic dialectic, inflicts upon the System a mortal wound . . . from behind, fighting the System and Speculation in order to show that 'the way' is not from the simple to the System and Speculation, but from the System and Speculation back again to the simple thing of becoming a Christian, fighting for this cause and vigorously slashing through to find the way back.

* The consecration, in so far as it dated from an earlier time, consisted in the resolution before God that, even if I were never to attain the goal of becoming a Christian, I would employ all my time and diligence to getting it made clear at least what Christianity is and where the confusions in Christendom lie—a labour for which I had prepared myself substantially from my earliest youth. Humanly speaking, that was surely a magnanimous undertaking. But Christianity is a power far too great to be willing as a matter of course to make use of a man's magnanimous resolution (which in my case was for the most part an expression of my relationship to my father), wherefore Christianity or Governance took the liberty of so arranging my subsequent life that there could be no misunderstanding (as indeed there was not from the beginning) as to whether it was I that stood in need of Christianity, or Christianity that stood in need of me.

So we have not to do here with a one-time aesthetic author who subsequently turns away from the world and the world's wisdom; he may rightly be said to have had from the earliest time quite exceptional predispositions for becoming a Christian, but they were all dialectical. Nor does he feel at this instant any impulse to go farther than becoming a Christian. With his conception of this task, and with the consciousness he has how far he is from being perfect, he feels only an impulse to go farther in becoming a Christian.

In case the benevolent reader has read this little book, he now knows what sort of an author I am.* So it is I represent myself. Should it prove that the present age will not understand me—very well then, I belong to history, knowing assuredly that I shall find a place there and what place it will be. Humble as I am before God, I also know this—and at the same time I know it as my duty definitely not to suppress this in silence; for if pride and arrogancy in claiming something for oneself is an abomination to God, so too, and just as much so, is the cowardly fear of men which depreciates itself with mendacious modesty—I also know *who* (humanly speaking) I was (the past tense because it is in God's power, every day, and even to-day, to alter it), that (in respect to genius) extraordinary gifts were bestowed upon me.

With this present little book, which itself belongs to a bygone time, I conclude the whole authorship, and then as the author (not an author simply, but the

---

* For that I myself possess a more exact and purely personal interpretation of my life is a matter of course.

author of this whole 'authorship') I advance to meet the future. What may betide me in the immediate future I know not; how it will be in the following age when I have passed into history, that I know. But whatever it be that I know in this respect, it would be of no comfort to me, were I not in faith and confidence, though in humility and also in penitence, advancing to meet that future which is nearest of all and at every instant equally near—eternity. Suppose that, if I should live longer, time will deprive me of all, and suppose that the following age will make the fullest reparation—how can that really harm me, or how can it profit? The former does not harm me if I merely take care to be absent, and the latter will not profit me, since then I shall have become in the solemn sense of the word an 'absent one'.

CONCLUSION

I HAVE nothing further to say, but in conclusion I will let another speak, my poet, who when he comes will assign me a place among those who have suffered for the sake of an idea, and he will say:

'The martyrdom this author suffered may be briefly described thus: He suffered from being a genius in a provincial town. The standard he applied in relation to talents, industry, disinterestedness, devotedness, definition of thought, &c., was on the average far too great for his contemporaries; it raised the price on them too terribly, and reduced their price too terribly; it almost made it seem as if the provincial town and the majority in it did not possess *dominium absolutum*, but that there was a God in existence. So for a while, at the first, people entertained one another mutually with voluble discussions about how under the sun he got such extraordinary talents, why he should have independent means and at the same time be able to be so industrious—that they disputed about for so long a time (while at the same time they took offence at one or another singularity in his mode of living, which, however, was not singular but very singularly calculated to serve the purpose of his life)—so long they disputed, that in the end it came to this: "It is his pride, everything can be explained by his pride." Thereupon they went farther, from disputation to action. Since it is his pride, they said, every insidious opposition, every insolence towards him or maltreatment of him is not only permissible but is a duty to God—it is his pride that should be punished. O priceless market town! How inestimable thou art when attired in thy comical dressing-gown and in the way of becoming holy, when abandonment to every disgusting inclination of envy, rudeness, and vulgarity becomes an expression of the worship of God! But how about his pride? Did the pride consist in the great talents? That would be like reproaching the golden sparrow by saying that it was its pride or because of its pride that it wears its golden finery. Or was it his diligence, &c.? If a child who had been very strictly brought up were to study in a class together with others, would it not be strange to say that his diligence, &c., was pride, even if it were the case that the others could not keep up with him? But such a case seldom occurs, for then the child is moved up to a higher class. But, unfortunately, for one who is in many ways developed for eternity's class there exists only one class, that of the temporal order, where perhaps he must remain a long while.

'This was the martyrdom. But therefore I, his poet, perceive also the epigram, the satire (not the one or the other which he wrote, but that which his whole life expressed) in the fact that now when all the "real" men with whom he (especially when legs[30] are the criterion—not for what it is to be a beast, *animal*, but for what it is to be a man) could not stand any comparison, that now when their legs like his are mouldering in their graves, and he has arrived in eternity (where, in parenthesis be it said, legs do not decide anything, neither their thinness nor their thickness) where (in parenthesis be it said) he is for ever dispensed, praise God, from being in company with bestiality, I see all these real men united heartily in one chorus, singing the peerless song of a provincial town which discourses only about what it understands, namely, his trousers which became "what the age requires", or, more precious still, a chorus which ironizes . . . the ironizer—I have only to think of this, and I cannot but burst out laughing. But in eternity it consoles him that he has suffered this, that he had exposed himself voluntarily to it, that he had not bolstered up his cause by any illusion, did not hide behind any illusion, but with God-fearing shrewdness transmuted his sufferings into a treasure for eternity: the memory of sufferings endured, and of fidelity to himself and to his first love, beside whom he has loved only them that have suffered in this world. Humble as he is, he will not with shame of face advance to meet those glorious ones who enjoy their reward in eternity—not with shame of face, as he would have approached them had his earthly life expressed the conviction that their life must have been either a casual happening, or a falsehood, or a proof of immaturity, since he by serving the truth had gained great honour and reputation, had everywhere encountered spiritual affinity and understanding, whereas they on the contrary encountered almost everywhere bestiality and misunderstanding.

'Yet it is true that he found also here on earth what he sought. He himself was "that individual", if no one else was, and he became that more and more. It was the cause of Christianity he served, his life from childhood on being marvellously fitted for such a service. Thus he carried to completion the work of reflection, the task of translating completely into terms of reflection what Christianity is, what it means to become a Christian. His purity of heart was to will only one thing. What his contemporaries complained of during his lifetime, that he would not abate the price, would not give in, this very thing is the eulogy pronounced upon him by after ages, that he did not abate the price, did not give in. But the grand enterprise he undertook did not infatuate him. Whereas as author he had dialectically a survey of the whole, he understood Christianly that the whole signified his own education in Christianity. The dialectical structure he brought to completion, of which the several parts are whole works, he could not ascribe to any man, least of all would he ascribe it to himself; if he were to ascribe it to any one, it would be to Governance, to whom it was in fact ascribed, day after day and year after year, by the author, who historically died of a mortal disease, but poetically died of longing for eternity, where uninterruptedly he would have nothing else to do but to thank God.'

'THE INDIVIDUAL'

TWO 'NOTES' CONCERNING MY WORK AS AN AUTHOR

By

S. KIERKEGAARD

Published in 1859 along with 'The Point of View'

PREFACE

IN these times politics is everything. Between this and the religious view the difference is heaven-wide (*toto caelo*), as also the point of departure and the ultimate aim differ from it *toto caelo*, since politics begins on earth and remains on earth, whereas religion, deriving its beginning from above, seeks to explain and transfigure and thereby exalt the earthly to heaven.

An impatient politician who hurriedly peeps into these pages will find little to edify him; so be it. Yet I am convinced that even he, if only he would be so kind as to bestow upon himself a little patience, will become aware, by merely the brief suggestions communicated in these pages, that the religious is the transfigured rendering of that which the politician has thought of in his happiest moment, if so be that he truly loves what it is to be a man, and loves people really, although he is inclined to regard religion as too lofty and ideal to be practical.

This judgement cannot discompose the religious man, who knows well that Christianity is and is commonly called the practical religion, and knows too that the 'Pattern', and all the relative patterns constantly being formed in correspondence with it, each of them individually, attained, at the cost of many years of exertion, of labour, of disinterestedness, the end of becoming as nothing in this world, of being derided, mocked, &c., which to a politician may seem the highest degree of unpracticality, whereas even a pagan, and precisely that 'practical philosopher' of antiquity,[31] was one who declared himself head over heels in love with *this* unpracticality.

But 'unpractical' as he is, the religious man is nevertheless the transfigured rendering of the politician's fairest dream. No politics ever has, no politics ever can, no worldliness ever has, no worldliness ever can, think through or realize to its last consequences the thought of human equality (*Menneske-Lighed*). To realize complete equality in the medium of worldliness (*'Verds-Lighed'*), i.e. to realize it in the medium the very nature of which implies differences, and to realize it in a worldly (*'verds-ligt'*) way, i.e. by positing differences—such a thing is for ever impossible, as is apparent from the categories. For if complete equality were to be attained, worldliness would be at an end. But is it not a sort of obsession on the part of worldliness that it has got into its head the notion of wanting to enforce complete equality, and to enforce it by worldly means . . . in a worldly medium? It is only religion that can, with the help of eternity, carry human equality to the utmost limit—the godly, the essential, the non-worldly, the true, the only possible human equality. And therefore (be it said to its honour and glory) religion is the true humanity.*

And one word more, if that be allowed me. What the age demands—who would ever get through with reckoning that out, seeing that now worldliness has caught fire by spontaneous combustion due to the friction of worldliness against worldliness? What, however, the age *needs* in the deepest sense can be said fully and completely with one single word: it needs . . . eternity. The misfortune of our time is just this, that it has become simply nothing else but 'time', the temporal, which is impatient of hearing anything about eternity; and so (with the best of intentions or furiously) would make eternity quite superfluous by means of a cunningly devised counterfeit, which, however, in all eternity will not succeed; for the more one thinks oneself to be able, or hardens oneself to be able, to get along without the eternal, the more one feels the essential need of it.

S. K.

[* A serious play on words was made possible here by the fact that in Danish the word for human equality is *Menneskelighed* (literally, human-likeness), and that worldliness is *Verdslighed* (world-likeness)—revealing what the English suffix obscures. Hence the argument: world-likeness emphasizes the differences and inequalities between man and man; the essential likeness and equality between men is apparent only before God, i.e. in religion; hence religion, since it establishes essential human equality, is humane in the highest sense, and as such is the realization of the fairest dream of the statesman who loves men and desires to affirm that 'A man's a man for a' that'.]

NO. 1

CONCERNING THE DEDICATION TO
'THE INDIVIDUAL'* 1846

MY dear, accept, I pray, this homage. 1 make it blindfold as it were, but therefore sincerely, undisturbed by respect of persons. Who thou art I know not, where thou art I know not, what thy name is I know not. Yet thou art my hope, my joy, my pride; although unknown thou art an honour to me.

It comforts me that the favourable occasion now presents itself to thee, which is what I sincerely intended during my labour and by it. For not then, when it had become the fashion, if such a thing were possible, for people to read what I write, or at least to make out that they had read it for the sake of gaining something in the world, not then would be the favourable occasion, then rather would misunderstanding triumph, and it would have deceived me also, if I had not striven to prevent such a thing from happening.

This, in part, is a possible change in me—something I welcome—attributable to a disposition of mind and soul which claims to be neither more than

---

* This, now revised and considerably enlarged, was written and intended to accompany the dedication to 'that individual' which is found in *Edifying Discourses in Various Spirits*. Copenhagen, 1847 (spring).

this nor less than this, but instead an admission: in part, it is a well-thought-out view of 'Life', of 'the Truth', and of 'the Way' [32]

There is a view of life which conceives that where the crowd is, there also is the truth, and that in truth itself there is need of having the crowd on its side.* There is another view of life which conceives that wherever there is a crowd there is untruth, so that (to consider for a moment the extreme case), even if every individual, each for himself in private, were to be in possession of the truth, yet in case they were all to get together in a crowd—a crowd to which any sort of *decisive* significance is attributed, a voting, noisy, audible crowd—untruth would at once be in evidence.†

For a 'crowd' is the untruth. In a godly sense it is true, eternally, Christianly, as St. Paul says,[33] that

* Perhaps it may be well to note here once for all a thing that goes without saying and which I never have denied, that in relation to all temporal, earthly, worldly matters the crowd may have competency, and even decisive competency as a court of last resort. But it is not of such matters I am speaking, nor have I ever concerned myself with such things. I am speaking about the ethical, about the ethico-religious, about 'the truth', and I am affirming the untruth of the crowd, ethico-religiously regarded, when it is treated as a criterion for what 'truth' is.

† Perhaps it may be well to note here, although it seems to me almost superfluous, that it naturally could not occur to me to object to the fact, for example, that preaching is done or that the truth is proclaimed, even though it were to an assemblage of hundreds of thousands. Not at all; but if there were an assemblage even of only ten—and if they should put the truth to the ballot, that is to say, if the assemblage should be regarded as the authority, if it is the crowd which turns the scale—then there *is* untruth.

'only one attains the goal'—which is not meant in a comparative sense, for comparison takes others into account. It means that every man can be that one, God helping him therein—but only one attains the goal. And again this means that every man should be chary about having to do with 'the others', and essentially should talk only with God and with himself—for only one attains the goal. And again this means that man, or to be a man, is akin to deity.— In a worldly and temporal sense, it will be said by the man of bustle, sociability, and amicableness, 'How unreasonable that only one attains the goal; for it is far more likely that many, by the strength of united effort, should attain the goal; and when we are many success is more certain and it is easier for each man severally.' True enough, it is far more *likely*; and it is true also with respect to all earthly and material goods. If it is allowed to have its way, this becomes the only true point of view, for it does away with God and eternity and with man's kinship with deity. It does away with it or transforms it into a fable, and puts in its place the modern (or, we might rather say, the old pagan) notion that to be a man is to belong to a race endowed with reason, to belong to it as a specimen, so that the race or species is higher than the individual, which is to say that there are no more individuals but only specimens. But eternity which arches over and high above the temporal, tranquil as the starry vault at night, and God in heaven who in the bliss of that sublime tranquillity holds in survey, without the least sense of dizziness at such a height, these countless multitudes of men and knows each single individual by name—He, the great Examiner, says that only one attains the goal. That means, every one can and every one should be this *one*—but only one attains the goal. Hence where there is a multitude, a crowd, or where decisive significance is attached to the fact that there is a multitude, *there* it is sure that no one is working, living, striving for the highest aim, but only for one or another earthly aim; since to work for the eternal decisive aim is possible only where there is one, and to be this one which all can be is to let God be the helper—the 'crowd' is the untruth.

A crowd—not this crowd or that, the crowd now living or the crowd long deceased, a crowd of humble people or of superior people, of rich or of poor, &c.— a crowd in its very concept* is the untruth, by reason of the fact that it renders the individual completely impenitent and irresponsible, or at least weakens his sense of responsibility by reducing it to a fraction. Observe that there was not one single soldier that dared lay hands upon Caius Marius—this was an instance of truth. But given merely three or four women with the consciousness or the impression that they were a crowd, and with hope of a sort in the

* The reader will also remember that here the word 'crowd' is understood in a purely formal sense, not in the sense one commonly attaches to 'the crowd' when it is meant as an invidious qualification, the distinction which human selfishness irreligiously erects between 'the crowd' and superior persons, &c. Good God! How could a religious man hit upon such an inhuman equality! No, 'crowd' stands for number, the numerical, a number of noblemen, millionaires, high dignitaries, &c.—as soon as the numerical is involved it is 'crowd', 'the crowd'.

possibility that no one could say definitely who was doing it or who began it—then they had courage for it. What a falsehood! The falsehood first of all is the notion that the crowd does what in fact only the *individual* in the crowd does, though it be every *individual*. For 'crowd' is an abstraction and has no hands: but each individual has ordinarily two hands, and so when an individual lays his two hands upon Caius Marius they are the two hands of the individual, certainly not those of his neighbour, and still less those of the . . . crowd which has no hands. In the next place, the falsehood is that the crowd had the 'courage' for it, for no one of the individuals was ever so cowardly as the crowd always is. For every individual who flees for refuge into the crowd, and so flees in cowardice from being an individual (who had not the courage to lay his hands upon Caius Marius, nor even to admit that he had it not), such a man contributes his share of cowardliness to the cowardliness which we know as the 'crowd'.—Take the highest example, think of Christ—and the whole human race, all the men that ever were born or are to be born. But let the situation be one that challenges the individual, requiring each one for himself to be alone with Him in a solitary place and as an individual to step up to Him and spit upon Him—the man never was born and never will be born with courage or insolence enough to do such a thing. This is untruth.

The crowd is untruth. Hence none has more contempt for what it is to be a man than they who make it their profession to lead the crowd. Let some one approach a person of this sort, some individual—

that is an affair far too small for his attention, and he proudly repels him. There must be hundreds at the least. And when there are thousands, he defers to the crowd, bowing and scraping to them. What untruth! No, when it is a question of a single individual man, then is the time to give expression to the truth by showing one's respect for what it is to be a man; and if perhaps it was, as it is cruelly said, a poor wretch of a man, then the thing to do is to invite him into the best room, and one who possesses several voices should use the kindest and most friendly. That is truth. If on the other hand there were an assemblage of thousands or more and the truth was to be decided by ballot, then this is what one should do (unless one were to prefer to utter silently the petition of the Lord's Prayer, 'Deliver us from evil'): one should in godly fear give expression to the fact that the crowd, regarded as a judge over ethical and religious matters, is untruth, whereas it is eternally true that every man can be the *one*. This is truth.

The crowd is untruth. Therefore was Christ crucified, because, although He addressed himself to all, He would have no dealings with the crowd, because He would not permit the crowd to aid him in any way, because in this regard He repelled people absolutely, would not found a party, did not permit balloting, but would be what He is, the Truth, which relates itself to the individual.—And hence every one who truly would serve the truth is *eo ipso*, in one way or another, a martyr. If it were possible for a person in his mother's womb to make the decision to will to serve the truth truly, then, whatever his martyrdom turns out to be, he is *eo ipso* from his mother's womb a martyr. For it is not so great a trick to win the crowd. All that is needed is some talent, a certain dose of falsehood, and a little acquaintance with human passions. But no witness for the truth (ah! and that is what every man should be, including you and me)—no witness for the truth dare become engaged with the crowd. The witness for the truth— who naturally has nothing to do with politics and must above everything else be most vigilantly on the watch not to be confounded with the politician—the God-fearing work of the witness to the truth is to engage himself if possible with all, but always individually, talking to every one severally on the streets and lanes ... in order to disintegrate the crowd, or to talk even to the crowd, though not with the intent of forming a crowd, but rather with the hope that one or another individual might return from this assemblage and become a single individual. On the other hand the 'crowd', when it is treated as an authority and its judgement regarded as the final judgement, is detested by the witness for the truth more heartily than a maiden of good morals detests the public dance-floor; and he who addresses the crowd as the supreme authority is regarded by him as the tool of the untruth. For (to repeat what I have said) that which in politics or in similar fields may be justifiable, wholly or in part, becomes untruth when it is transferred to the intellectual, the spiritual, the religious fields. And one thing more I would say, perhaps with a cautiousness which is exaggerated. By 'truth' I mean always 'eternal truth'. But politics, &c., have nothing to do with 'eternal truth'. A policy which in the proper sense of 'eternal truth' were to make serious work of introducing 'eternal truth' into real life would show itself in that very same second to be in the most eminent degree the most 'impolitic' thing that can be imagined.

A crowd is untruth. And I could weep, or at least I could learn to long for eternity, at thinking of the misery of our age, in comparison even with the greatest misery of bygone ages, owing to the fact that the daily press with its anonymity makes the situation madder still with the help of the public, this abstraction which claims to be the judge in matters of 'truth'. For in reality assemblies which make this claim do not now take place. The fact that an anonymous author by the help of the press can day by day find occasion to say (even about intellectual, moral, and religious matters) whatever he pleases to say, and what perhaps he would be very far from having the courage to say as an individual; that every time he opens his mouth (or shall we say his abysmal gullet?) he at once is addressing thousands of thousands; that he can get ten thousand times ten thousand to repeat after him what he has said—and with all this nobody has any responsibility, so that it is not as in ancient times the relatively unrepentant crowd which possesses omnipotence, but the absolutely unrepentant thing, a nobody, an anonymity, who is the producer (*auctor*), and another anonymity, the public, sometimes even anonymous subscribers, and with all this, nobody, nobody! Good God! And yet our states call themselves Christian states! Let no one say that in this case it is possible for 'truth' in its turn by the help of the press to get the better of lies and errors. O thou who speakest thus, dost thou venture to maintain that men regarded as a crowd are just as quick to seize upon truth which is not always palatable as upon falsehood which always is prepared delicately to give delight?—not to mention the fact that acceptance of the truth is made the more difficult by the necessity of admitting that one has been deceived! Or dost thou venture even to maintain that 'truth' can just as quickly be understood as falsehood, which requires no preliminary knowledge, no schooling, no discipline, no abstinence, no self-denial, no honest concern about oneself, no patient labour?

Nay, truth—which abhors also this untruth of aspiring after broad dissemination as the one aim— is not nimble on its feet. In the first place it cannot work by means of the fantastical means of the press, which is the untruth; the communicator of the truth can only be a single individual. And again the communication of it can only be addressed to the individual; for the truth consists precisely in that conception of life which is expressed by the individual. The truth can neither be communicated nor be received except as it were under God's eyes, not without God's help, not without God's being involved as the middle term, He himself being the Truth. It can therefore only be communicated by and received by 'the individual', which as a matter of fact can be every living man. The mark which distinguishes such a man is merely that of the truth, in contrast to the abstract, the fantastical, the impersonal, the crowd—the public which excludes God as the middle term (for the *personal* God cannot be a middle term in an *impersonal* relationship), and thereby excludes also the truth, for God is at once the Truth and the middle term which renders it intelligible.

And to honour every man, absolutely every man, is the truth, and this is what it is to fear God and love one's 'neighbour'. But from an ethico-religious point of view, to recognize the 'crowd' as the court of last resort is to deny God, and it cannot exactly mean to love the 'neighbour'. And the 'neighbour' is the absolutely true expression for human equality. In case every one were in truth to love his neighbour as himself, complete human equality would be attained. Every one who loves his neighbour in truth, expresses unconditionally human equality. Every one who, like me, admits that his effort is weak and imperfect, yet is aware that the task is to love one's neighbour, is also aware of what human equality is. But never have I read in Holy Scripture the commandment, Thou shalt love the crowd—and still less, Thou shalt recognize, ethico-religiously, in the crowd the supreme authority in matters of 'truth'. But the thing is simple enough: this thing of loving one's neighbour is self-denial; that of loving the crowd, or of pretending to love it, of making it the authority in matters of truth, is the way to material power, the way to temporal and earthly advantages of all sorts—at the same time it is the untruth, for a crowd is the untruth.

But he who acknowledges the truth of this view, which is seldom presented (for it often happens that a man thinks that the crowd is the untruth, but when it—the crowd—accepts his opinion *en masse*, everything is all right again), admits for himself that he is weak and impotent; for how could it be possible for an individual to make a stand against the crowd which possesses the power! And he could not wish to get the crowd on his side for the sake of ensuring that his view would prevail, the crowd, ethico-religiously regarded, being the untruth—that would be mocking himself. But although from the first this view involves an admission of weakness and impotence, and seems therefore far from inviting, and for this reason perhaps is so seldom heard, yet it has the good feature that it is even-handed, that it offends no one, not a single person, that it is no respecter of persons, not a single one. The crowd, in fact, is composed of individuals; it must therefore be in every man's power to become what he is, an individual. From becoming an individual no one, no one at all, is excluded, except he who excludes himself by becoming a crowd. To become a crowd, to collect a crowd about one, is on the contrary to affirm the distinctions of human life. The most well-meaning person who talks about these distinctions can easily offend an individual. But then it is not the crowd which possesses power, influence, repute, and mastery over men, but it is the invidious distinctions of human life which despotically ignore the single individual as the weak and impotent, which in a temporal and worldly interest ignore the eternal truth—the single individual.

NOTE. The reader will recall that the foregoing (the beginning of which bears the impress of that instant when

I voluntarily exposed myself to the rough treatment of literary vulgarity)B was originally written in 1846, although later it was revised and considerably enlarged. Since that time actual events,[34] almighty as they are, have cast light also upon this thesis, that the crowd, ethico-religiously regarded as the supreme authority, is the untruth. Verily, this accrues to my advantage. For my own part, I have been helped by it to secure my own position and to understand myself; and at the same time I am sure now to be very much better understood than at that time when my weak and solitary voice was heard as a ludicrous exaggeration— whereas now it is hardly to be heard at all by reason of the loud tones with which actual events speak to the same effect.

NO. 2

A WORD ABOUT THE RELATION OF MY LITERARY ACTIVITY TO 'THE INDIVIDUAL'*

A TRIFLE is condemned to lead a despised and neglected life, as everybody knows—but it takes its revenge. For what is it but a trifle that lies at the bottom of every misunderstanding, especially if it is passionate and ill tempered? Otherwise it would not be a misunderstanding at all, but an essential disagreement. What constitutes a misunderstanding is the fact that what one party regards as significant the other regards as insignificant, and this by reason of the fact that at bottom they are separated by a trifle, that the parties who are in disagreement through a misunderstanding have not taken the time to understand one another at the start. For at the bottom of all real disagreement there is an understanding. The *groundlessness* of 'misunderstanding' is due to the lack of a preliminary understanding, without which both agreement and disagreement are alike a misunderstanding. Therefore it is possible for misunderstanding to be removed and become agreement and understanding; but it is possible also for it to be removed and to become real disagreement. For there is no misunderstanding involved in the fact that two persons really disagree. They really disagree just because they understand one another.

I am surely not far at fault when I assume that

* This article was written in 1847 but was later revised and enlarged.

what has occasioned and still continues to occasion disagreement between certain of my contemporaries and me with respect to my activity as an author is in part 'that individual'. No doubt several of them would read my works if it were not for this, and the crowd would leave me entirely at peace if it were not for this.

If this matter of 'that individual' were a trifle to me, I could let it drop; indeed, I should be delighted to do so and should be ashamed if I were not willing to do it with the most obliging alacrity. But such is far from being the case. For me—not personally, but as a thinker—this matter of the individual is the most decisive thing. So then the only possibility left is to remove the misunderstanding. If I could succeed in making it evident to the individuals that it truly is no trifle, then in that case the disagreement also would be removed. For what occasions the confusion is the fact that people regard it as a trifle—and then are indignant that I should attach so much importance to a trifle. One of two things therefore: either the others are right about its being a trifle, and I ought to give it up; or it is, as I understand it, something very essential, and so there is no ground for complaining that I attach so much importance to something that is essentially important. On the contrary there is good ground for a little serious reflection about its importance. What I, for my part, ought not to have neglected to do I did not neglect. Once upon a time[B] (in a little article by Frater Taciturnus in the *Fatherland*)* I let the thing be carried as far as possible in

* One will remember moreover that this was a pseudonym,

the direction of singularity—verily not out of queer singularity on my part. On the contrary, the significance of what I did was clear to me in the highest degree, and I acted responsibly, with a full sense of my responsibility for doing what it would have been irresponsible of me not to do. I let that be done (and had it printed in a newspaper, moreover, and in an article moreover which touched upon the beginning and the end of the town gossip) because it seemed to me important to get attention provokingly fixed upon that point, which is something one does not accomplish by ten books which develop the doctrine of the individual, nor in ten lectures which deal with it, but accomplishes in these times only by getting the laughter aimed at one* by making people a bit angry so as to make them upbraid one again and again and without ceasing for that very thing which one would wish to have emphatically accentuated and, if possible, brought to the attention of all. This is absolutely the surest sort of tutorial coaching. But any one who desires to accomplish anything must know the age in which he lives and then have courage to encounter the danger of employing the surest means.

This means I have employed, though the dialectic

and that accordingly the difficulty of writing a polemical article was increased by the poetical form I had to adopt to be consistent with the character of the pseudonym.

* And (rightly understood) between me and laughter there is a secret and happy understanding. I am (rightly understood) a friend and lover of laughter, and in a sense (that is, in all seriousness) never more truly so than just at that moment when the others, all these thousands and thousands, became ironical, and I (ironically enough) was the only one that had no understanding of irony.

of 'the individual' was constantly made ambiguous by its duplex movement. In every one of the pseudonymous works this theme of 'the individual' comes to evidence in one way or another; but there the individual is predominantly the pre-eminent individual in the aesthetic sense, the distinguished person, &c. In every one of my edifying works the theme of 'the individual' comes to evidence, and as officially as possible; but there the individual is what every man is or can be. The starting-point of the pseudonyms is the difference between man and man with respect to intellect, culture, &c.; the starting-point of the edifying works is the edifying thought of the universal human. But this double meaning is precisely the dialectic of 'the single individual'. 'The single individual' can mean the one and only, and 'the single individual' can mean every man. So if one would provoke attention dialectically, one should use the category of 'the individual' with a double lash to it. The pride in the one thought incites some, the humility in the second thought deters others, but the confusion involved in the double meaning provokes attention dialectically; and, as I have said, this double meaning is precisely the thought of 'the individual'. But I believe that people have for the most part paid attention only to 'the individual' of the pseudonyms and have confounded me as a matter of course with the pseudonyms—and hence all this talk of my pride and arrogance, a condemnation of me which really amounts only to self-denunciation.

This phrase, 'that individual', has by this time been accentuated almost to the point of becoming a proverb—and I—poor me!—have had to put up with the laughter. If I had begged with tears and adjured everybody by all that is holy and for the sake of God in heaven to pay attention to this thought of eternal value —surely nobody would have troubled himself about it.

Now that it has been duly accentuated I will make an attempt, with all the powers at my command, to remove the misunderstanding, at least in part. This is a misunderstanding, however, which can exist only for one who has not made himself acquainted in a deeper sense with my works. And the desire to prevent all misunderstanding about an enterprise one is about to undertake is a thing that could occur only to a youth. There is nothing that so easily gets beyond one's control and so easily becomes misunderstood, as a misunderstanding. Even if one were to undertake nothing more than merely to avoid misunderstanding—then in that case one would presumably become the most thoroughly misunderstood of all men.

I know, of course, quite well that I have had from the first much more than one reader. 'Denmark is a little land'; its inhabitants, having their own peculiar language, are not numerous; with respect to literature the conditions are so petty that there does not now exist, nor has there for a long time existed, such a thing as a literary review, but literature was reduced (*ad absurdum*) to such attention as the daily press and more especially Merchant Nathanson[35] (to use his own words) 'bestowed upon it'. As an author I have laboured with unusual diligence and unusual speed, in the service of the truth I have constantly expended a lot of strength and a lot of inventiveness, I do not say to prevent the circulation of my works, but to prevent their circulation under a misapprehension; and when this is taken into account, I have many more readers than might be expected. This I know quite well, and I who know it am not at all ungrateful; and perhaps I have shown my gratitude in a truer and more honest way by never abusing this fact as a means of enticing more purchasers and readers. Therefore the notion that on my side there might be something to prevent me from desiring that my popular works should if possible be read and understood by all— this notion is one that only foolishness and ill temper[36] could hit upon and only envy could use in order the more to confuse people already confused (which only too easily succeeds, as a matter of course), and in order if possible to embitter against me the well disposed, the better sort, the more competent— which is not quite a matter of course, and which— God be praised!—has failed of success in a measure quite beyond my expectation, so that the fact that just the opposite has occurred is for me a truly edifying joy.

Every serious person who has any eye for the conditions of our time will easily perceive how important it is to make a profound effort and a rigorously consistent one, which does not draw back from the extreme consequences of the truth, to oppose boldly the immoral confusion which, philosophically and socially, tends to demoralize 'the individual' by means of 'mankind' or a fantastical notion of society; a confusion which proposes to teach ungodly contempt for that which is the prime condition of religiousness, namely, to be a single individual man. This confusion can only be opposed by making men if possible single individuals—yet after all every man is a single individual! Every serious person who knows what edification is—every one, whether he be high or low, wise or simple, man or woman, every one who has felt himself edified and God brought near to him—will unconditionally agree with me that it is impossible to edify or be edified *en masse*, even more impossible than to be 'in love *en quatre*'[37] or *en masse*. Edification, even more expressly than love, is related to the individual. The individual—not in the sense of the specially distinguished or the specially gifted individual, but the individual in the sense in which every man, absolutely every man, can be and should be—should take pride in being, but verily will also discover his blessedness in being . . . an individual. Every individual among the many who have read something in my edifying works and found edification in it, every one upon whom I, as an edifying author, have had some influence—if in a quiet hour of meditation he will put to himself the question (as he ought to do for his own sake, he being the judge, and also perhaps for my sake who often have had to be judged in a place where it is not exactly wisdom that is judge) whether I deceived him with this talk about 'the individual', whether I deceived him by exposing myself for a while to the laughter of the many*

---

* I shall not dwell here upon the fact that beside the reason adduced in this place there were others, and among

and to the purposes for which envy could desire to use this laughter; he surely will rather admit, if not to me (which I do not require), yet to himself, that what is lacking to him is that he has not yet rightly become the single individual, which is something I do not pretend to be, although I have striven, without yet apprehending,[38] and continue to strive, yet as one who does not forget that 'the individual' in its highest measure is beyond a man's power.

'The individual' is the category through which, in a religious respect, this age, all history, the human race as a whole, must pass. And he who stood at Thermopylae was not so secure in his position as I who have stood in defence of this narrow defile, 'the individual', with the intent at least of making people take notice of it. His duty was to prevent the hosts from pressing through the defile. If they pressed through, he was lost. My task is one which at least does not expose me to any such danger of being trampled underfoot, for my task was as a humble servant (yet, as I have said from the beginning and repeated again and again, 'without authority') to

them this consideration, that it was for the sake of making my generation aware if possible of a literary immorality which reached out only too frightfully in all directions, that I, a self-immolated man, ventured to be for a while—alas, poor Master of Irony!—a sacrifice to that laughter, which, however (for are not irony and sadness truly one and the same thing?), filled my soul with a deep sadness with respect to one thing; for what they call the common people have hardly had many in Copenhagen who loved them in a Christian way more sincerely than I did—naturally enough, for I have been neither a journalist nor an agitator.

provoke, if possible, to invite, to stir up the many to press through this defile of 'the individual', through which, however, no one can pass except by becoming the individual—the contrary being a categorical impossibility. And yet, if I were to desire an inscription for my tombstone, I should desire none other than 'That Individual'—if that is not now understood,* it surely will be. The pseudonyms in their time, when here at home all the talk was about system, always system, aimed a blow at the System† with the category of 'the individual'. Now one hardly hears the System any more mentioned‡—not at least as the last word of fashion and as the requirement of the age. I marked the beginning of the literary production over my own name by the category of 'the individual', and that remained as a stereotyped formula, showing that this thing of the individual is not a later invention of mine but my first thought. With the category of 'the individual' is bound up any ethical importance I may have. If that category was right, if that category was in place, if I saw rightly at this point and understood rightly that it was my task (certainly not a pleasant nor a thankful one) to call attention to it, if that was the task given me to do, albeit with inward sufferings such as certainly are

* The reader will remember that this was written in 1847. The world-upheaval of 1848 has brought understanding considerably nearer.

† And every one who has even a little dialectic will perceive that it is impossible to attack the System from a point within the System. But outside of it there is only one point, truly a spermatic point, the individual, ethically and religiously conceived and existentially accentuated.

‡ And now in 1848!

seldom experienced, and with outward sacrifices such as a man is not every day found willing to make—in that case I stand fast and my works with me.

That category, the fact of having used that category, and of having used it so personally and so decisively, is ethically the conclusive thing. Without this category, and without the use that has been made of it, reduplication would be lacking in my whole activity as an author. For from the fact that in the works there was said, presented, developed, and declared all that actually is declared there, and that, too, perhaps with imagination, dialectic, psychological insight and other such qualities—it would not by any means follow from this as a matter of course that the author had understood, and understood how to express by one single word with absolute finality (while by his action he expressed his understanding of his age and of himself in it), **that this was an age of dissolution.***

For proclaiming this the author does not call himself 'a witness for the truth'. No, far from it! This name is not to be applied to every one who says something true—no, in this way we should have more than enough witnesses for the truth. No, to discern 'a witness for the truth' his personal mode of existence must be ethically examined in relation to what he says, to see if the personal existence is an expression of what he says—though this is a consideration which the systematizing and lecturing tendency and the general

* With regard to this estimate of the present age compare, among other passages, the second part of *A Literary Review*, by S. K., Copenhagen 1846.

want of character in our generation has set aside. Now it is true that the author's life has expressed with tolerable precision the aim he ethically defined as that of being an individual. He has had acquaintance with countless people, but always has stood alone, and with all his striving he strove among other things for permission to stand alone, whereas in the environment committees were pretty nearly everything—setting them up, setting them down, and setting them aside. He has also made more than one sacrifice for the sake of his category, has exposed himself to one danger after another, and, be it observed, to just the kind of danger which categorically corresponds to 'the individual', i.e. he has exposed himself to 'the crowd' and to 'the public'. But even if there were nothing else in the way (of the claim that he is 'a witness for the truth') there is the fact that he was not compelled to work for his living. That alone is enough, it is a privilege which puts him down in a lower class. But beside that, he has had too much imagination and far too much of the poet about him to dare to be called in a stricter sense a witness for the truth. At the beginning he was very far from having a survey of the whole, so that it was only gradually he learnt to understand himself as having apprehended rightly. Hence he has had to lay to heart the wise saying which Lessing[39] so happily expresses, 'Let us not be wise where we have merely been fortunate', he has had occasion to remember the duty of giving unto God the things that are God's. He has had too much to do with the ethical to be a poet. The issue of his life recalls the first word of the aesthetic writer in *Either/Or*, which was repeated later, about not desiring to be a poet,* and it recalls the emphasis with which the ethical writer† approves of this, recognizing that a man must get out of the poetical and into the existential, the ethical.‡ And yet he is too much of a poet to be a witness for the truth. He is between the two as a border line, which, however, is related with categorical precision to history in its future stage.

'The individual' is the category of the spirit, of spiritual awakening, a thing as opposite to politics as well could be thought of. Earthly reward, power, honour, &c., have no connexion with the right use of this category. For even if it is used in the interest of the established order, inwardness does not interest the world; and when it is used catastrophically, it still does not interest the world, for to make sacrifices, or to be sacrificed (which may in fact be the consequence of declining to entertain the thought of becoming a power of a material sort), does not interest the world.

* Cf. *Either/Or*, 1st Diapsalm, p. 3; cf. also p. 23, 'In vain I strive against it. My foot slips. My life must yet become a poet-existence', &c. [The page-references in this and the following notes is to S. V. 2nd ed.]

† Cf. *Either/Or*, Part Two, p. 227; cf. the *Concluding Postscript*, p. 238.

‡ The movement from 'the poet' to religious existence is substantially the movement of my whole activity as an author integrally understood. One may compare *The Works of Love*, II. A and B, with regard to the use which again is made of 'the poet' as *terminus a quo* for Christian religious existence. With regard to the movement described in a series of works as *away from* the philosophical, the systematic, to the simple, i.e. the existential, it is essentially the same movement as from the poet to religious existence.

132

'The individual'—that is the decisive Christian category, and it will be decisive also for the future of Christianity. The fundamental confusion, the original sin, of Christendom is that year after year, decade after decade, century after century, it has pursued the insidious purpose—just about half unconscious of what it would, and essentially unconscious of what it did—of tricking God out of his rights as the proprietor of Christianity, and has got it into its head that the race, the human race, was itself the inventor, or had come pretty close to inventing Christianity. Just as in civil law a fortune reverts to the state when it has lain unclaimed for a certain period of years and no heir presents himself—so has the race, perverted by observation of the trivial fact that Christianity is a thing that actually exists, thought within itself as follows: 'It is now so long a time since God has let Himself be heard from as proprietor and master that Christianity has consequently reverted to us, who can either decide to abolish it altogether, or to modify it *ad libitum*, very much as we might deal with our own possession or invention, treating Christianity, not as something which *in obedient subservience to God's majesty* **must** be believed, but as something which in order to be acceptable must try by the aid of *reasons* to satisfy "the age", "the public", "this distinguished assembly", &c.' Every revolt in science . . . against moral discipline, every revolt in social life . . . against obedience, every revolt in political life . . . against worldly rule, is connected with and derived from this revolt against God with respect to Christianity. This revolt—the abuse of 'the human race' as a category—does not, however, resemble the revolt of the Titans, for it is in the sphere of *reflection*, insidiously carried out from year to year, from generation to generation. Reflection constantly takes only a tiny little bit at a time, and about this little bit one can constantly say, 'Why, in small matters one may well yield'—until in the end reflection will have taken everything without anybody noticing it, because it came about little by little, 'and in small matters one may surely yield'. Hence men must become single individuals in order to get the proper Christian-pathetic impression of Christianity. The individual, every individual, will surely beware of initiating a legal process against God in heaven to determine which of the two, absolutely and unto the least tittle, has the right of proprietorship in Christianity. God must again become effectually the middle term. But to God as the middle term corresponds the individual. If the 'race' is to be the court of last resort or even have subordinate jurisdiction, Christianity is abolished—if in no other way, at least by the *wrong and unchristian form* one gives the *Christian* message. Not even the most trusted spy of the shrewdest detective agency can more confidently vouch for the content of his report than I, a mere private practitioner, a spy *si placet*, will vouch for the correctness of this.

'The individual'—with this category the cause of Christianity stands or falls, since world-development has got so far along in reflection as it has. Without this category pantheism has triumphed absolutely. Men will surely come who will know how to strain this category dialectically to a higher tension—they have not had the labour of bringing it to notice. But the category of 'the individual' is and remains the fixed point which is able to resist the pantheistic confusion, it is and remains the weight which turns the scale. But those who work and operate with this category must be more and more dialectical in proportion as the confusion is greater and greater. For one can guarantee to make a Christian of every man he can get to come under this category—in so far as one man can do this for another, or we may say rather, that he can vouch for it that such a man will become a Christian. As a single individual he is alone, alone in the whole world, alone before God—and with that there is no question about obedience! All doubt (which, be it observed parenthetically, is just simply disobedience to God—when it is ethically considered and not made a fuss about with an air of scientific superiority)—all doubt has ultimately its stronghold in the illusion of temporal existence that we are a lot of us, pretty much the whole of humanity, which in the end can jolly well overawe God and be itself the Christ. And pantheism is an acoustic illusion which confounds *vox populi* with *vox dei*, an optical illusion, a cloud-picture formed out of the mists of temporal existence, a mirage formed by reflection from temporal existence and regarded as the eternal. But this category cannot be delivered in a lecture; it is a specific ability, an art, an ethical task, and it is an art the practice of which might in his time have cost the practitioner his life. For that which in God's eyes is the highest thing, the self-willed race and the hosts of confused minds regard as *lèse-majesté* against 'the race', 'the crowd', 'the public', &c.

'The individual'—this category was used only once with decisive dialectical force, and for the first time, by Socrates[40] to dissolve paganism. In Christendom on the other hand it will serve a second time to make men (i.e. Christians) into Christians. It is not the category of the missionary who deals with pagans to whom he proclaims Christianity for the first time; but it is the category of the missionary within Christendom itself, aiming to introduce Christianity into Christendom. When he, 'the Missionary', comes, he will use this category. For if this age awaits a hero, it awaits him in vain. There will sooner come one who in godly weakness will teach men obedience . . . for the fact that they in ungodly revolt put him to death who was obedient to God, who meanwhile used this category, though on an infinitely greater scale—and 'with authority'. But no more of this. I remain grateful to Providence—both in the one sense and in the other sense—for what, as is readily seen, is in every respect infinitely subordinate, namely, to call attention to this category.

POSTSCRIPT

What is said here is said about the past, the time gone by, as the reader will have observed, if only because of the tenses used. And the category is, 'to call attention', which I here repeat for the sake of doing to the very last all that I can do to prevent misunderstanding.

(1849.)

REGARDING THE 'TWO NOTES'

A POSTSCRIPT

March 1855.

ON re-reading these two articles now I would add what follows.

It is perfectly true that (to mention the highest instance) the Truth itself, Jesus Christ, had disciples; and (to mention a human instance) that Socrates had disciples.

So it seems, in a sense, that I force the ideality of the individual even higher than they did. How do I understand that? In part I understand it as an imperfection in me, and in part as connected with the singularity of my task. I understand it as my imperfection, for my whole activity as a writer, as I have often said, was at the same time my own education, in the course of which I have learnt to reflect more and more deeply upon my idea, my task. But as long as such was the case with me, I was not yet, even if I had wished it, sufficiently ripe to be able to draw individuals nearer to me. I understand this as connected with the singularity of my task. For my task is to oppose a given factor wrongly promulgated—so it is not to promulgate something on my own account, rather, I might say, it is to be a smoke-consumer. But in such a case it is important to be cautiously on one's guard about forming intimate relationship with individuals, lest the smoke-consumer attain in his turn a false promulgation. It is not my task, and in Christendom it cannot rightly be the task, to create a lot of titular

Christians or to assist in confirming the millions in the illusion that they are Christians. No, the task is in precise terms to throw light upon the knavish trick, which for the advantage of church dignitaries, of parsons, of mediocrity (under the name of Christian ardour and zeal—Oh, how subtle!) has brought these millions into being. The point is to illuminate this knavish trick through and through, and to get it made clear that 'in Christendom' Christian ardour and zeal mean just this thankless task (and here we have the note which characterizes Christian activity, just as profit characterizes worldly activity) of liberating Christianity from some of these battalion-Christians.

Only one word more. It is perfectly true that Christ had disciples, and (to take a human instance) that Socrates also had disciples; but not in any sense that would make my thesis false did either Christ or Socrates have disciples—ethically and ethico-religiously the crowd is untruth, the untruth of wishing to work by means of the crowd, the numerical, of wishing to make the numerical the criterion which decides what truth is.

MY ACTIVITY AS
A WRITER

By

S. KIERKEGAARD

Copenhagen 1851

Wer glaubt, der ist gross und reich,
Er hat Gott und das Himmelreich.
Wer glaubt, der ist klein und arm,
Er schreiet nur: Herr, Dich erbarm!

[TERSTEGEN: Der Frommen Lotterie]

THE ACCOUNTING

Copenhagen, March, 1849.

WHEN a land is little the proportions are in every respect small in the little land. So in respect to literature: the honorarium and all that goes with it will be insignificant. If one is not a poet, and more particularly a dramatist, and does not write text-books or is not supported in some other way by one's profession, then the business of being an author is about the most wretchedly rewarded, the least secure, and so to that extent the most thankless occupation. If there live a man possessed of the talents requisite for authorship, who in addition to that is so fortunate as to have some property, he can then become an author more or less at his own expense.[41] However, this is fitting enough and therefore constitutes no ground for complaint. It is becoming for the individual in his particular calling to love his idea, the nation to which he belongs, the cause which he serves, and the language in which as an author he has the honour to write. Such indeed will be the case when there is harmony of understanding between the individual and the people, which in turn (if such be the case) will treat the individual rather handsomely.

Whether my experience has been in any respect the contrary of this,[42] whether I may have been treated unhandsomely by one or many—that is, properly speaking, something which does not concern me, but is very properly their concern. On the other hand, what does concern me, and what I so gladly acknowledge as my concern, is to have the duty and privilege of rendering thanks for what favour, good-will, friendliness, and appreciation have been shown me in general or by particular individuals.

The movement described by the authorship is this: *from* the poet (from aesthetics), *from* philosophy (from speculation), *to* the indication of the most central definition of what Christianity is—**from** the *pseudonymous* 'Either/Or', **through** 'The Concluding Postscript' *with my name as editor*, **to** the 'Discourses at Communion on Fridays',* two of which were

---

* Later, however, there appeared a new pseudonym, Anti-Climacus. But the very fact that he is a pseudonym indicates (as the name *Anti*-Climacus itself indicates) that he is rather to be regarded as a signal of arrest. All the earlier pseudonyms are lower than the 'edifying author'; the new pseudonym represents a higher pseudonymity. It is to be understood, however, that the 'arrest' is accomplished by pointing out a higher ideal, with the consequence of forcing me back within the bounds of my limitations, condemning me because my life does not correspond to so lofty a claim, so that of necessity the communication is a poetic one.—And somewhat earlier there appeared a little book, *Two Minor Ethico-Religious Treatises*, by H. H. Without going further into the question than I would, it is not easy to explain the significance of this little book, which does not so much belong *in* the authorship as *to* the authorship regarded as a whole, and hence was made anonymous for the sake of keeping it quite outside. It is like a nautical beacon *towards* which one steers, but in such a way, be it observed, that the navigator understands he *has to keep a certain distance away from it*. It defines the limitations of the authorship. 'The Difference between a Genius and an Apostle' (treatise No. 2) is that 'the genius is without authority'. But just because genius as such is without authority it lacks entirely the ultimate concentration in itself which bestows power and title to emphasize the duty of

delivered in the Church of our Lady. This movement was accomplished or described *uno tenore*, in one breath, if I may use this expression, so that the authorship, *integrally* regarded, is religious from first to last—a thing which every one can see if he is willing to see, and therefore ought to see. And as the natural scientist at once recognizes by the way the strands are crossed in the spider's web what artful little animal it is who made the web—so the discerning mind will recognize that corresponding to this authorship there is an originator who, as author, 'has only willed one thing'.* The discerning mind will at the same time recognize that this one thing is the religious, but the religious altogether and utterly transposed into reflection, yet in such a way that it is altogether and utterly withdrawn from reflection and restored to simplicity—that is to say, he will see that the road travelled has the aim of *approaching*, *of attaining* simplicity.

'letting oneself be put to death for the truth' (treatise No. 1). Genius as such remains in the sphere of reflection. That again is the category of my whole authorship: to *call attention* to the religious, more specifically to Christianity—but *without authority*.—And finally, to take account of even the least things, there appeared later *The Lilies of the Field and the Birds of the Air*, three godly discourses, which served as the accompaniment to the second edition of *Either/Or*: and also *The High Priest—The Pharisee—The Woman that was a Sinner*, three discourses at Communion on Fridays, which served as the accompaniment to Anti-Climacus' *Sickness unto Death*—both of which little works repeat the first preface, the Preface to the *Edifying Discourses* of 1843.

October 1849.

* Referring to the theme of one of his discourses, entitled *Purity of Heart*—which is to will one thing.

And this, moreover, is the **Christian** movement (a movement in *reflection*, as in fact it originally was). In a Christian sense simplicity is not the point of departure from which one goes on to become interesting, witty, profound, poet, philosopher, &c. No, the very contrary. *Here* is where one begins (with the interesting, &c.) and becomes simpler and simpler, *attaining* simplicity. This, in 'Christendom', is the Christian movement: one does not reflect oneself into Christianity; but one reflects oneself out of something else and becomes, more and more simply, a Christian. If the author had been a richly gifted mind, or (supposing him to be that) if he had been doubly as gifted a mind, he would have needed a longer, or doubly as long a time, to follow out this path in his literary production and to reach this point.

But just as that which has been communicated (the religious thought) has been translated entirely into terms of reflection and again taken back out of reflection, so the *form of communication* also has been decisively marked by reflection; in other words, use has been made of the kind of communication which is appropriate to reflection. 'Direct communication' means to communicate the truth directly. 'Communication in terms of reflection' means to beguile a person into the truth. But since the aim of the movement is to attain simplicity, the communication must, sooner or later, end in direct communication. It began *maieutically*, with aesthetic works * and all the pseu-

* The maieutic attitude lies in the relationship between aesthetic works as a beginning and religion as τέλος. The

donymous works are *maieutic*. That indeed is the reason why these works were pseudonymous—whereas the direct religious communication (which was present from the very first as a glinting suggestion) bore my own name. Direct communication was present from the first, for the 'Two Edifying Discourses' of 1843 were actually simultaneous with 'Either/Or'.* And in order to establish this direct religious communication definitely as contemporaneous, each new pseudonym was accompanied almost simultaneously by a little collection of *Edifying Discourses*—until the appearance of the *Concluding Postscript*, which set the problem, which is the Problem κατ᾽ ἐξοχήν, of the whole authorship, namely, 'how to become a Christian'.†

point of departure was the aesthetic, wherein possibly the majority have their being; and then the religious is introduced so unexpectedly that they who were moved to follow along by the attraction of aesthetics suddenly find themselves in the midst of the most decisive definitions of Christianity and are obliged at least to take notice.

* At the same time this disposes of the illusion that religion is something one has recourse to as one grows older. 'One begins as an aesthetic writer, and then, when one has grown older, and no longer possesses the vigour of youth, one becomes a religious writer.' But when an author begins *simultaneously* as an aesthetic and a religious author, it surely is not possible to explain the religious works from the casual circumstance that he has grown older; for simultaneously one surely cannot be older than oneself.

† The *situation* (i.e. to become a Christian in 'Christendom', when one is naturally a 'Christian'), a situation which, as any dialectician can perceive, translating everything into terms of reflection, makes necessary at the same time the use of indirect communication, because the aim in this case is to disabuse men of an illusion which consists in calling themselves Christians, perhaps imagining that they are, without being any such thing. And so the man who set the

From that moment the glinting hints of direct religious communication cease and there begins the purely religious productivity: *Edifying Discourses in Divers Spirits*; *The Works of Love*; *Christian Discourses*. But as a reminder of the beginning (and corresponding to the position occupied by the *Two Edifying Discourses* at the beginning, when the majority of the writings were aesthetic) there came at the conclusion (when for a long time the productivity had been exclusively and voluminously religious) a little aesthetic article by *Inter et Inter* in the daily edition of the *Fatherland*, for July 1848, Nos. 188–99. Coming at the beginning, the *Two Edifying Discourses* had hinted, like a preliminary flash, that this was really what was to come out of it all, the goal to be attained. The flash of the little aesthetic article, coming as it does at the conclusion, by reflecting as it were the hint given at the beginning of the authorship, draws attention to the fact that from the very beginning the aesthetic was merely the point of departure, a position which had to be left behind. The *Concluding Postscript* is the middle point, and that so precisely (though this is not worthy to be mentioned except as a curiosity) that even the quantity of the matter presented before and after is roughly equal—

problem did not describe himself *directly* as a Christian and the others as not being such; *on the contrary*, he denied that he was one and conceded it to the others. This is what Johannes Climacus does.—Where pure receptivity is concerned, like the empty vessel which is to be filled, direct communication is in place; but where illusion enters in, that is to say, when there is something that must be got rid of, direct communication is out of place.

if, as is only reasonable, the *Eighteen Edifying Discourses* are included in the purely religious work; and even the time occupied by the authorship before the *Concluding Postscript* and after it is about the same.

Finally, in another respect also the movement of the authorship is decisively characterized by reflection, or rather it is the movement of reflection itself. The direct way of beginning is with individuals, some few readers; and then the business is—or rather the direction of the movement—to assemble a crowd, to win for oneself an abstraction, the Public. Here, on the contrary, the **beginning** was made, *maieutically*, sensationally, and with what naturally accompanies that, namely, the Public—which is always at hand when there is something going on—and the movement was, maieutically, to stir up the 'crowd' in order to get hold of 'the individual',* understanding this

* This again (corresponding to the fact that a religious author *begins* with aesthetic production, and to the fact that, instead of loving himself and his own advantage, and forwarding his effort by creating illusion, he hates himself and removes the illusions)—this again, I say, is the dialectical movement, or is essentially dialectics, namely, in one's *action* to *counteract* oneself at the same time, which is what I call reduplication, and it is an example of the heterogeneity which distinguishes every true godly effort from worldly effort. To strive or to work *directly* is to work or to strive in immediate continuity with an actually given condition. The dialectical movement is the exact *opposite* of this, namely, by one's action to counteract one's effort at the same time—a duplication which is 'seriousness', like the pressure upon the plough which determines the depth of the furrow, whereas the direct effort is a slurring over, which not only goes more quickly and easily, but is by far a more thankful task, for it is worldliness and homogeneity.

word in a religious sense. Precisely at the same
moment when the sensation awakened by *Either/Or*
was at its height, there appeared the *Two Edifying
Discourses* of 1843, which employed the formula subsequently repeated as a stereotyped phrase: 'It seeks
that single individual whom with joy and gratitude I
call my reader.' And precisely at the critical moment
when the *Concluding Postscript* (which, as I have said,
sets the Problem) was delivered to the printer, with
instructions to begin the work as soon as possible, and
the publication presumably was bound to follow
shortly—just at that moment one of the pseudonyms
in a newspaper article, directed at the spot where it
would be most effective, made the greatest possible
effort to repel the public,* and thereupon began the
decisive religious production. I attached myself again
religiously to 'that individual', to whom the next
essential† work (after the *Concluding Postscript*) was
dedicated. I refer to *Edifying Discourses in Divers
Spirits*, or rather the first part of that book which is an

---

* Only one thing more. The journal of literary despica-
bleness[43] had attained a frightfully disproportionate circulation. Speaking in all sincerity, I believed that what I did
was at the same time a charitable deed. It was rewarded
(even by some of those for whose sake I exposed myself to
such treatment) . . . as a work of love commonly is rewarded
in this world, and by help of such reward it became a truly
Christian work of love.

† For the little literary review of the novel *Two Generations* followed so immediately upon the *Concluding Postscript*
that it is all but contemporaneous. As a matter of fact, it is
one of the things I produced *qua* critic, not *qua* author;
yet in the last section it contains, from the point of view of
'the individual', a sketch of the future which the year 1848
did not belie. [See note C.]

148

exhortation to confession. Perhaps nobody noticed it the first time I employed the category 'that individual', and nobody paid much attention to the fact that it was repeated in stereotyped form in the preface of every number of the Edifying Discourses. When for the second time, or in a second potency, I reiterated the message and stood firmly by my first pronouncement, everything was done that could be done to lay the whole weight of emphasis upon that category. Here again the movement tends towards simplicity: it is from the public to the individual. *Religiously* speaking, there is no such thing as a public, but only individuals;* for religion is seriousness, and seriousness is . . . the individual—in the sense, however, that every man, absolutely every man, inasmuch as he is a man, can be, indeed must be, an individual. To me, the edifying author, it was and is, therefore, a joy that from this very time there were several who became attentive to this matter of 'the individual'. This was and is a joy to me; for though it is true enough that I have faith in the rightness of my thought against all the world, yet almost the last thing for me to relinquish is my faith in individual men. And this is my faith, that however much there may be that is confused and evil and detestable in men who have become that irresponsible thing without possibility of repentance which we call the 'public', the 'crowd', there is just as much truth and goodness

* And in so far as there is, in a religious sense, such a thing as a 'congregation', this is a concept which does not conflict with 'the individual', and which is by no means to be confounded with what may have *political* importance: the public, the crowd, the numerical, &c.

and loveliness in them when one can get hold of the individual. Oh! and in what a high degree would men become—men, and lovable men, if they would become individuals before God!

So it is that I understand everything *now*. From the beginning I could not thus survey what has been in fact my own development. Prolixity of statement would nowhere be more out of place than here. What is here required is to be able to fold together in simplicity that which is unfolded in the many books, or as unfolded constitutes the many books; and this brief communication is more particularly occasioned by the fact that the first-fruit of authorship now comes forward a second time, namely, the second edition of *Either/Or*, which I was unwilling to publish earlier.

Personally—when I bethink me of my inward sufferings, as well as of my personal offences—one thing concerns me absolutely, is more important to me than the whole authorship, and lies closer to my heart, namely, to express, as sincerely and as strongly as possible, what I can never be sufficiently grateful for, and what, when once I have forgotten the whole authorship, I shall unalterably and for ever remember—how infinitely much more Providence has done for me than I ever had expected, could have expected, or might have dared to expect.

Without authority to **call attention** to religion, to Christianity, is the category for my whole activity as an author, integrally regarded. That I was 'without authority' I have from the first moment asserted clearly and repeated as a stereotyped phrase. I regarded myself preferably as a *reader* of the books, not as the *author*.

'Before God', religiously, when I talk with myself, I call the whole literary activity my own upbringing and development—not, however, implying that I am now perfect or completely finished so as to need no more upbringing and development.

MY POSITION AS A RELIGIOUS WRITER IN 'CHRISTENDOM' AND MY TACTICS

I

MY POSITION

Copenhagen, November 1850.

I HAVE never fought in such a way as to say: I am the true Christian, others are not Christians. No, my contention has been this: *I know what Christianity is*, my imperfection as a Christian I myself fully recognize—but I know what Christianity is. And to get this properly recognized must be, I should think, to every man's interest, whether he be a Christian or not, whether his intention is to accept Christianity or to reject it. But I have attacked no one as not being a Christian, I have condemned no one. Indeed, the pseudonym Johannes Climacus, who sets the problem 'about becoming a Christian', does exactly the opposite: he denies that he is a Christian and concedes this claim to the others—the remotest possible remove, surely, from condemning others! And I myself have from the first clearly asserted, and again and again repeated, that I am 'without authority'. And again, finally, in the last book of Anti-Climacus (which especially in Part I, by the help of a poetic treatment which ventures to say everything and of a dialectic which shrinks from no consequences, has endeavoured to unsettle the illusions), no one, absolutely no one is condemned. The only person named, whom it attacks, by saying that in trying to realize the ideals he is but a very imperfect Christian, is myself—the only one condemned (cf. the thrice repeated Preface). This I can well put up with, for I am infinitely concerned that the requirements of the ideal may at least be heard. But this again is surely at the remotest remove from condemning others.

2

MY TACTICS

The tactics in use for a long time past have been to employ every means to get as many as possible, and if possible all, to enter into Christianity—but without being at all scrupulous to ascertain whether what one got them to go into was really Christianity. My tactics were, by God's aid, to employ every means to make it clear what the requirement of Christianity truly is—even though not one single person should be induced to enter into it, and though I myself might have to give up being a Christian (in which case I should have felt obliged to make open admission of the fact). On the other hand, my tactics were these: instead of giving the impression, in however small a degree, that there are such difficulties about Christianity that an apology for it is needed if men are to be persuaded to enter into it, rather to represent it as a thing so infinitely lofty, as in truth it is, that the apology belongs in another place, is required, that is to say, of us for the fact that we venture to call ourselves Christians, or it transforms itself into a contrite confession that we have God to thank if we merely assume to regard ourselves as Christians.

But neither must this ever be forgotten: Christianity is just as lenient as it is austere, just as lenient, that is to say, infinitely lenient. When the infinite requirement is heard and upheld, heard and upheld in all its infinitude, then *grace* is offered, or rather grace offers itself, and to it the individual, each for himself, as I also do, can flee for refuge. And then it is possible. But surely it is not an exaggeration when (in the interest of grace itself) the requirement of infinity, the 'infinite' requirement, is presented infinitely. Exaggeration occurs only when, in an entirely different way, the requirement is presented and grace is not even alluded to. On the other hand, it is taking Christianity in vain when (perhaps in consideration of the claim—which presumably will over-awe both God in heaven and Christianity and the Apostles and martyrs and witnesses to the truth and the fathers, with all their *praxis*—that 'this won't do at all in practical life')— Christianity is taken in vain, when in view of this considera-tion the infinite requirement is reduced to finite terms, or maybe entirely ignored, and 'grace' is introduced *as a matter of course*, which simply means that it is taken in vain.

But never, even in the remotest way, have I made as if I wished to develop a pietistic severity, which is a thing alien to my soul and nature. Never have I wanted in the least to over-tax human existences, for that is a thing which would distress the spirit within me. No, I have desired to be instrumental in bringing, if possible, by means of admissions, a little more truth into the imperfect existences which we lead (pointing in the direction of ethical and ethico-religious character, the renunciation of worldly wisdom, readiness to suffer for the truth, &c.), which after all is something, and is at any rate the first condition for learning to live more effectively. What I have desired to prevent is, that one who has limited himself to the easier and lower should thereupon 'go farther'[44] and abolish the higher, go farther and put the lower in its place, go farther and represent the higher as a fantastic and ludicrous exaggeration, the lower as wisdom and true seriousness—to prevent any one in 'Christendom' from taking Luther and the significance of Luther's life in vain. This I have desired to be instrumental, if possible, in preventing.

What was needed among other things was a Godfearing satire. This I have prevented, especially by the aid of the pseudonyms, which have not let me go scot-free by any means. But in order that there might be no possibility of confusion, that this satire might not be confounded with a thing which is only too prone to give itself out as satire: the profane revolt of the most deeply sunken Power—it was I, I who had presented that godly satire, that flung myself against and exposed myself to that profane satire of slave-revolt.[B] Thus in the first place I have striven in godly fear to be honest. And then, though a sting of the truth is contained in the propositions, everything nevertheless is made as lenient as possible, seeing that there is talk only of admissions and concessions, and indeed only of such concessions and admissions as every one is left free to make for himself before God.[45] Yet this very leniency is perhaps in another sense vexatious to some. It would be much easier to be rid of the whole thing if the author were a scatterbrain who at every point exaggerated both the accusation and the requirement. And although this is not the case, one and another might contrive to spread the report that it was so. But by God's help this effort will fail. If I were in fact a strong ethico-religious character—alas! I am indeed hardly more than a poet!—and if I were consequently entitled and constrained in virtue of the truth to speak more sternly, it is plausible to suppose that instead of finding favour with my *contemporaries* I might encounter opposition. But since I am not so strong, I surely must succeed in finding favour with my *contemporaries*—not consequently because of my perfection, as a sense of truth obliges me to admit.

With regard to the 'established order', then, seeing that my special concern was 'the individual', which was the point of my polemic against the numerical, the crowd, &c., I have always done the very opposite of attacking it; I have never been in or with the 'opposition' which wants to get rid of the 'government',[46] nor have I been allied with it; but I have furnished what may be called a 'corrective', the intent of which was: For God's sake let us continue to be ruled by those who are appointed and called to this task, and that they should stand fast in the fear of God, willing only one thing, the Good. And thereby I have managed to fall out with the opposition and the public, and have encountered moreover once in a while the disapprobation of one and another (perhaps not well informed) official of the bureau-cracy. In so far as the church establishment understands itself, it will in the same degree understand also the last book, *Training in Christianity*, as an attempt to provide an idealistic support for the establishment. In the first instance I did not wish to speak out directly,* as I do here (what, as a matter of fact, the Preface expresses directly by expressing how I understand the book) in order, in the interest of truth, not to spare myself in the face of a situation which, probable or improbable, was always a possibility;[47] in order not to evade the difficulties and dangers which might arise if the establishment were to undertake to convert my com-munication into opposition—which would have prompted serious misgivings about the state of the establishment's health. Thank God, this did not occur, however. Yet it is quite possible that some well-informed office-bearer—to whom the fact that I have no official position was in itself

---

* That the book (except for the Editor's Preface, which stands by itself) is a defence of the established order cannot be affirmed *directly*, since the form of communication is doubly reflected; it might equally well be the very reverse, or be understood as such. 'Directly' I only say, therefore, that an established order which understands itself must understand the book thus; all doubly reflected communica-tion makes contrary interpretation equally possible, and the judge will be made manifest by his judgement.

reproach enough—might have perpetrated the ludicrous folly of rushing forward to defend and shield the establishment against what at this moment is surely a possible defence of the establishment, so long as it understands itself.

In '48 the strands of the web of worldly wisdom broke.[c] The shrill rasping note which announces chaos became audible! 'This was the year '48, it stood for progress.' Yes . . . if only a 'government' is consolidated. For that, perhaps, not a single new official is necessary, nor the discharge of any old one, but perhaps an inward transformation which would consolidate the state in the fear of God. The fault from above was clearly this, that throughout the government, taken as a whole, from top to bottom, the strength relied upon was essentially worldly shrewdness, which essentially is nothing more than lack of strength. The fault from below was that they wanted to get rid of government, that is to say, of punishment. But the punishment fits the crime, and the punishment now is that the want most bitterly felt at this time is simply the want of a government. Never as in our century was the race and the individual within it (the ruler and the ruled, the superior and the inferior, the teacher and the taught, &c.) so emancipated from all restraint (so to call it) due to the idea that there is something which unconditionally stands fast. Never has the race and the individual within it discovered so deeply that the race itself and every individual within it needs and craves to have something which unconditionally stands fast. Never have 'opinions' (the most heterogeneous, in the most various fields) felt themselves, under 'Liberty, Equality, and Fraternity', so free, so unhampered, so fortunate, with the rule of go as you please which is expressed in the motto, 'up to a certain point'. Never will the race and the individual within it discover so deeply that it and every individual within it needs and craves to have something which stands and shall stand unconditionally fast, craves for that which the loving Godhead in love discovered, namely, the unconditional; in the place of which man, who is shrewd to his own undoing, in admiration for himself, posited this admired maxim, 'up to a certain point'. Require the navigator to sail without ballast—he capsizes. Let the race, let each individual, make the experiment of doing without the unconditional—it is a whirlpool and remains such. In the meanwhile, for a longer or a shorter period, it may seem otherwise, it may seem like stability and security. But at bottom it is and remains a whirlpool. Even the greatest events and the most laborious lives are whirlpools, or they are like sewing without knotting the thread—until the end is once again made fast by the fact that the unconditional is brought to bear, or that the individual, however remotely, comes to relate himself to the unconditional. To live in the unconditional, inhaling only the unconditional, is impossible to man; he perishes, like the fish forced to live in the air. But on the other hand, without relating himself to the unconditional, man cannot in the deepest sense be said to 'live'. He gives up the ghost—that is, he may continue perhaps to live, but spiritlessly. To stick to my subject, the religious, I say that the race, or a considerable number of the individuals within the race, have outgrown the childish notion that another person can represent the unconditional for them and in their stead. Very well; but for all that, the unconditional does not cease to be necessary. Rather it is the more necessary the more the individual outgrows childish dependence upon other men. Hence 'the individual' himself must relate himself to the unconditional. This is what I, in proportion to the talents granted to me, with the utmost expenditure of effort, and with many sacrifices, have consistently fought for, fighting against every tyranny, including that of the numerical. This effort of mine has been interpreted as hatred, as monstrous pride and arrogance—I believed and still believe that this is Christianity and love for one's 'neighbour'.

TWO FRAGMENTS FROM
KIERKEGAARD'S *JOURNAL*

As has been remarked above in the Preface, Kierkegaard never ceased to debate with himself over the validity of his motives and the character of his mission. The two statements below are offered as a small but poignant sample of the extensive entries interpreting his authorship and his relations to his Governance. The order of their appearance here deliberately violates chronology in order to suggest a representative cycle of the swings of Kierkegaard's moods and attitudes.

The first passage was inscribed in his *Journal* six days after the appearance of *My Activity as a Writer* (7 August 1851). Kierkegaard's mood seems one of determined self-assurance. Perceiving himself a champion in a battle whose tide was now turning, he cheerfully announces the start of a new phase of his campaign. Yet in the background there are traces of a desire to convince himself that his 'accounting' of his personal and literary career was proof against the mild qualification of Bishop Mynster,* and the repeated observation of one of his reviewers that 'the author considers his authorship essentially finished'.

The second passage, which bears the date '1849', presents the author in a less decisive and confident frame of mind. Instead, he seeks with brooding earnestness to correct certain exaggerations in the tone and argument of his *Point of View*. He regrets having allowed others and himself to suppose that he was ending his activity as a writer in expectation of his early death as a martyr. He deems himself fortunate that 'The Individual' had been withheld from publication. Mystery was at the core of his being, whether as Poet or as Penitent or as one who was perhaps 'Extraordinary' in the religious dimension. The greatest error either he or anyone else might make was to perceive him as a resolute person spurred by powerful and consistent ethical aims. It was for his Governance and not for himself to say who he was and what he was to do. Without humble trust in Divine guidance there was no escaping egocentric distortions in one's perception of one's relation to the Governance.

The rendering of these hitherto untranslated fragments from the *Journal* is by Mr. Lee M. Capel. The originals will be found at Vols. X⁴ A 383 and X¹ A 250, respectively, in *Søren Kierkegaards Papirer*, 2nd ed., by P. A. Heiberg, V. Kuhr and E. Torsting, Vols. I–XI³ (in 20 parts). Copenhagen: Gyldendalske Boghandel, Nordisk Forlag, 1909–48. (B. N.)

I

This little book is not a kind of authorship, a new composition, but a deed; it was therefore important that it be as short as possible, and that it not indicate a new productivity which people could talk about. This little book is a *metabasis eis allo genos* (transition to another sphere), and shows to what extent such a sphere was already present in my whole authorship.

Even if I had known or comprehended beforehand every detail of my authorship, what is here said about it should never have been said at the beginning; for this would have disturbed the perspective, and the literary world would have acquired the kind of interest which belongs to curiosity, namely, whether I really conformed to and fulfilled my predictions.

No, this book should come at the end and do in a single blow, what the sailor says of a battle: turn the tide.

This little book is not a literary production but a deed. It is an intensive deed which will not be understood at first, just as my affair with the *Corsair* was not understood in its day. Perhaps some will feel that I have not made enough of myself, I who might venture to give myself out to be a genius or a talent—but instead call it 'my own development and education'. But this is precisely the turn in the direction of Christianity and personality. . . .

Without this little book the whole authorship would become transformed into a new doctrine.

2

N.B. †

'The Three Notes' shall not be published.‡ There shall not be any direct discussion of myself; and if there should be, then much more should be said —if *The Point of View* should be published. Everything of this nature shall be finished as it is until after my death.

There shall not be anything said about my own person and in a direct way: (1) because I am nevertheless essentially a poet; but in a poet's personality there is always something mysterious, and this is the reason he must not be represented with, and, above all, not confuse himself with, an absolute ethical character in the strictest sense. (2) In so far as I am a little more than a poet, I am essentially a penitent; but of this I cannot speak, and consequently neither shall I speak of the possible extraordinary dimension which is given to me. (3) I can not guarantee either in the case of myself or the communication that the impression falls forcefully enough upon God. (4) This is an inconsistency in the direction of self-denial.

To want to do it, therefore, was on my part: (1) a thoughtlessness, in wanting now to speak of myself as if I should either die tomorrow or as if it were decided that I would cease to be an author, since neither alternative is the case. (2) It was an impatience or arbitrariness (the result of having suffered) myself to want to determine my fate beforehand, or contribute to forcing myself further into the character of a martyr—even though I am one in all stillness, yet without demanding the satisfaction of being so regarded.

It was a godsend that I did not do it, that I did not publish the 'Notes', or that God did not allow it to happen. In every way it would have disturbed my life—whether I shall now continue to be an author, or whether I am occupied in another way. Hence I must regret the time when I was foolishly occupied with the 'Notes'—now a word here, now a word there. I have suffered much, but God also helps me to learn.

How much God is the one who guides the whole I see best from the fact that the discourses about the lilies and the birds were written at that time—and that is precisely what I needed. God be praised! Without struggling with men and without speaking about myself I get much said that needs to be said—but inspiring, mild, and edifying.

And now to travel. I must get away from this place, both for a moment's recreation and for a longer period—this is related to the fact that I am essentially a poet.

If I should communicate directly about my person, I must be externally compelled to do it—and even then with difficulty, since the productivity is essentially not my own but that of a higher power.

NOTES

* Kierkegaard evidently drew Mynster into a conversation about *My Activity as a Writer* on 9 August 1851. Mynster remarked: 'Yes, there is a thread through the whole but spun later—but then you don't say any more than that yourself'. To which Kierkegaard replied: 'The essential thing to be observed is that through so many years and with so much productivity my pen has not made one single digression'. *Papirer*, X⁴ A 373.

† This abbreviation implies the placement of this entry in the *Nota Bene* section of the *Journal*, for which see W. Lowrie's *Kierkegaard*, II, in bibliographical appendix.

‡ Originally, 'The Individual' was to comprise three notes. Kierkegaard changed his plan and issued a shortened version of the projected third note as a Foreword to *Two Discourses at the Communion on Fridays* (1851), available in Dr. Lowrie's translation under the title *For Self-Examination and Judge for Yourselves!* (New York: Oxford University Press, 1941), pp. 1–26.

APPENDIX

NOTES BY THE TRANSLATOR

A. *The Story of an Unhappy Love*

IN 1837, when he was twenty-four years of age, S. K. met Regina Olsen, a beautiful girl of fourteen, and fell in love with her at first sight. However, on account of her tender years he did not make love to her till three years later, by which time his father had died and left him a considerable fortune. On 10 September 1840, when Regina was seventeen years of age, he won her promptly by his impetuous wooing. But no sooner were they engaged than he discovered a scruple about marrying. It was a religious obstacle, as he conceived it, though without doubt it must be attributed to his melancholy. He loved her warmly, but he conceived it to be his duty to break the engagement. He passed many dreadful months before he could make up his mind to send her back the ring (on 11 August 1841), and still more dreadful were the two months which ensued before he could persuade her to let him go. For during that time he pretended that he was a 'scoundrel' who had won her without loving her. He conceived that he must play this part in order to free her from her attachment to him and give her sufficient 'resiliency' to marry another. During these terrible months he wrote a great part of the second volume of *Either/Or*, which depicts the bliss of love on the moral basis of a married life. Taking refuge in Germany from the gossip of the town, he completed the whole book in an incredibly short time. Returning to Berlin on 8 May 1843, he came near to completing two other books: *Repetition* and *Fear and Trembling*. All of these works, like the *Two Edifying Discourses* with the dedication to 'that individual', were covertly addressed to Regina, with the hope that after all it might be possible to marry her. But on returning to Copenhagen he found that she was already engaged to Fritz Schlegel, a worthy young man to whom she had been half-engaged before she was won by S. K.— and the conclusion of these two books had to be radically altered accordingly. Though he had succeeded in his aim of giving her 'resiliency', he was profoundly discomfited by his success. He was faced then by the grimmest experience a man can know: 'the loss of the possibility'—and yet from the very depths he floated up again, getting the experience that he was lighter than water, that he could 'float above seventy thousand fathoms'. This was the religious experience which in *The Point of View* he stresses while he seems to ignore the experience of 'indescribable joy' at the moment of his conversion five years earlier. But Regina had made him a poet, and he continued at full speed to produce his pseudonymous works in amazing variety.

He continued to love 'Her' to the end of his life—and she, outliving him by many years, and outliving her husband, continued to love him. He had not succeeded in making her believe he was a scoundrel.

B. *The Affair of the 'Corsair'*

At the moment when S. K. had finished the manuscript of his prodigious book *The Concluding Postscript* (the turning-point of his authorship, as he regarded it), and had already sent it to the printer, he found himself at liberty to challenge the *Corsair* to a contest which resulted in consequences far more serious to him than he could have anticipated. I see no reason to doubt that he was justified in affirming, as he often did, that he voluntarily exposed himself to this danger for the good of the community. In his childhood he was already so 'highly polemical' that he never hesitated to engage in unequal combat with sturdier schoolmates. But in this case he doubtless expected that he would be sustained by the better elements in the community, and he often expresses his indignation that not one of the eminent men in Copenhagen raised a hand to support him against an adversary which they all reprobated.

The *Corsair* was a comic weekly owned and edited by a clever young Jew named Goldschmidt, who had a special admiration for S. K., by whom he had been treated with singular courtesy. This sheet, with the pretext that it was serving the ends of political liberalism by levelling down everything that was high in Denmark, was really a gross money-making affair which attained a larger circulation than any paper in the land by providing for the common people the delectable spectacle of the upper classes exposed to the vilest derision. Nobody of eminence felt safe from its attacks—except Kierkegaard, whom Goldschmidt had lately exalted as an 'immortal' writer. Undoubtedly such a paper threatened Denmark with moral dissolution, and S. K.'s attack upon it was a public-spirited as well as a courageous act.

S. K., who by his life on the streets came in contact with everybody and knew all that was going on, was aware that at that time, in 1845, 'the effectual editor' of the *Corsair* was P. L. Møller, a man whom he held in just contempt, but who was then seeking appointment to the professorship of literature in the University. This man in his annual literary review, *Gaea*, published a supercilious criticism of S. K.'s *Stages on Life's Road*, and S. K. promptly replied with a letter in a daily paper over the name of his pseudonym Frater Taciturnus, heaping contempt upon P. L. Møller and complaining that the *Corsair* had put him to humiliation by 'immortalizing' him, on the one hand, and on the other hand, by failing to include him among all the other eminent writers whom it abused. He demanded that he be promptly admitted to the pages of the *Corsair*, and in this connexion he revealed the secret of P. L. Møller's connexion with that disreputable paper. The blow was a mortal one for P. L. Møller, for it made it impossible for him to attain the university chair he coveted. He soon left the country and came to a miserable end in France. But Goldschmidt, after a vain gesture of reconciliation, suffered the storm to be let loose against S. K., and for the course of about a year almost every number of the *Corsair* carried one or more caricatures designed to make Denmark's greatest writer ridiculous in the eyes of the vulgar. And the vulgar hailed this 'irony' with such enthusiasm that the name of Søren became synonymous with everything that is ridiculous—not only in Denmark but throughout Scandinavia. The theme continually harped upon was the thinness of his legs and the unequal length of his trousers. His figure, as S. K. himself was ready to admit, lent itself only too readily to caricature. The superior people laughed in their sleeves—out of envy, as S. K. not unreasonably suspected. And even after Goldschmidt was moved by shame to put an end to his lucrative paper and leave Denmark for a while, the merriment which he had begun at S. K.'s expense still went on. Almost to the end of his life S. K. was pursued by the jibes of urchins on the street, and by the impudence of louts even on his frequent carriage excursions in the country. Thus his favourite recreations were embittered to him, and he was cut off from the solace he had enjoyed in friendly conversation with the common people, who naturally were shy of him when they had been taught to regard him as a half-crazy fool. This whole experience was a crucial one in S. K.'s life. After the rupture of his engagement it was the only external event which profoundly influenced him. But while it increased his unhappiness and isolation, it added, as he said, 'a new string to my instrument'. Among other things, it effectually deterred him from seeking refuge pusillanimously in a country parsonage.

Many readers of the *Journal* are impatient at S. K.'s constant complaints against this 'persecution of vulgarity' and are disposed to think that a man less morbidly sensitive would have paid no attention to it. For my part, when I see how far it went and how long it lasted, I am disposed to think that few men could have endured it with less show of ill-temper, and I agree with him in accounting his assault upon the 'despicable organ of vulgarity' a highly meritorious act of courage—perhaps of temerity.

C. *The Year 1848*

The frequent references in the text to the year 1848 have in view two things which were distinct and yet connected: (1) the war with Germany by which Denmark lost the provinces of Schleswig and Holstein; and (2) the bloodless political revolution which changed the absolute monarchy in Denmark into a constitutional one. It may seem to us exaggerated that S. K. should speak of either or both of these events as a 'world-upheaval'. Yet in fact it meant the tardy introduction into Denmark of the world-shattering theories of the French Revolution, and it was accompanied by violent upheavals in other parts of Europe.

CONSECUTIVE NOTES

1. By the tactics of 'indirect communication' and the cunning with which he preserved his incognito.

2. By 'reduplication' he means translating the truth intellectually apprehended into the terms of actual living ('existence').

3. His dissolute life prior to his conversion on 19 May 1838.

4. In the first place he meant it as a hint to Regina that he was addressing her particularly.

5. Aimed at Grundtvig, the leader of an enthusiastic party to which his brother Bishop Peter Kierkegaard belonged.

6. The followers of Grundtvig.

7. His first essay at an explanation of his works he entitled 'Armed Neutrality', but it was left uncompleted. *Papirer* x. 5 B 107–10, pp. 288–303. Cf. ix. B 64, 65.

8. Referring to Magister Adler, a clergyman who was deposed for claiming to write under direct inspiration from Jesus Christ. It was a case which profoundly engrossed the attention of S. K. and upon which he wrote a big book which he never published.

9. Rom. viii. 16.

10. The political situation in 1848. See note C.

11. The affair of the *Corsair*. See note B.

12. One of the editors of a conservative daily, the *Fatherland*, and an intimate friend of S. K.'s—in spite of the fact that he was a journalist.

13. The *Rhetoric*, iii. 18.

14. Goldschmidt, the owner of the *Corsair*.

15. An allusion to the fact that the degree of Magister Artium had been granted him for his able dissertation on 'The Concept of Irony'.

16. An allusion to his letter requiring the *Corsair* to admit him among the eminent persons whom it held up to ridicule.

17. One of the blackguards put forward as straw-men, i.e. as legally responsible editors who were paid to take the punishment for libel, &c.

18. M. Curtius of Roman legend.

19. The war with Germany in 1848 by which Denmark lost her southern provinces.

20. So he was called in Plato's *Phaedrus*.

21. Shakespeare's *Richard III*, v, scene ix. 4.

22. 1 Samuel, xv. 22.

23. 2 Cor. xii. 7.

24. 'Without authority' was first used in the Preface to the *Two Edifying Discourses* of 1843.

25. S. K.'s treatise on 'The Difference between a Genius and an Apostle'.

26. It is strange that he speaks here of the 'religious awakening' which he experienced in losing Regina and seems to ignore the conversion of 19 May 1838. See note A.

27. Cf. the prefaces to the *Fragments* and the *Postscript*.

28. This he said in several places in his journal was the consequence of his experience with the *Corsair*.

29. The open letter to P. L. Møller referred to in note 16, which demolished his adversary. See note B.

30. His thin legs and his trousers of unequal length were the themes upon which the cartoonist of the *Corsair* chiefly dwelt. See note B.

31. Socrates.

32. John xiv. 6.

33. 1 Cor. ix. 24.

34. The revolution of 1848.

35. Owner and editor of a liberal daily in Copenhagen called *Berlin Times*. He was a special object of S. K.'s detestation.

36. Referring to an utterance of P. L. Møller's in his reply to S. K.'s attack.

37. Cf. *The Concept of Irony*, S. V. xiii, p. 390.

38. Phil. iii. 12 f.

39. Lessing's *Emilia Galotti*, II. iv.

40. e.g. Plato's *Gorgias*: 'I know how to produce one person as a witness for what I say, viz., the person I am talking with. With the crowd, on the other hand, I do not concern myself.'

41. S. K. published his earlier works at his own expense, and it has been too readily assumed that he expended in this way a great part of his fortune. Lately it has been shown by Brandt that on the whole he received back more than he expended and that his later works were published on commission. His frequent complaints that he had been compelled 'to lay out money on his works' must be understood to mean that an author so industrious might justly expect to receive emoluments sufficient to support him altogether. Such would be the argument of any wage-earner.

42. He is thinking especially of his painful experience with the *Corsair*. See note B.

43. The *Corsair*. See note B.

44. Referring to Hegel's boast that the speculative philosopher, while accepting the substance of traditional Christianity, went farther, i.e., transcended the common understanding of it by a more adequate conception.

45. Referring to the Preface of *Training in Christianity*.

46. From his youth S. K. was recognized as a political conservative and was valued as such by the King and his government.

47. He means that his works had not been publicly condemned by Bishop Mynster or by any other ecclesiastical authority.

INDEX

Aesthetics, 6, 10 ff., 25 f., 30, 38 ff., 41, 45 ff., 73 f., 90, 146, 148, 150 f.
Anonymous, 44 f., 118 ff.
Anti-Climacus, 146, 159.
Apology (defence), 7, 51.
Apostle, 75, 146.
Authorship, 5, 9 ff., 44 ff., 64 ff., 85, 98, 123 ff., 145 f., 154.

'Before God', 7, 20, 97, 137, 155, 161.

'Call attention', 138, 155.
Childhood, 76 f.
Christendom, 22 ff., 25, 30 ff., 36, 42 f., 73 f., 77, 90, 96 f., 138, 148, 160.
Christian(s), 22 ff., 25 ff., 159.
Christian, becoming a, 6, 22, 29, 38, 41 f., 53, 74 f., 90, 93, 95 ff.
Christian Discourses, 62, 150.
Christianity, 6, 22 ff., 41, 77, 97, 159 f., 164.
Concluding Postscript, 13, 41 ff., 56, 75, 91, 97, 134, 146, 149 f., 152.
'Corrective', 162.
'Corsair', 57 f., 122, 152.
Country cure, 86.
Crowd, 47, 55, 59, 94, 112 ff., 138, 140, 151 f.

Deception, 38 f., 73, 90.
Development, my, 154 f.
'Diary of the Seducer', 19, 95.
Direct communication, 25 ff., 40, 93, 148 ff., 162.
Disciples, 139 f.

Discourses at Communion, 146.
Double reflection, 162.
Duplicity, 10 ff.

Edifying Discourses, 11 ff., 17 ff., 86, 147 ff.
Edifying Discourses in Various Spirits, 150, 152.
Either/Or, 5, 11 ff., 18 ff., 47, 49, 85, 96, 133 f., 146, 149, 152, 154.
Equality, 110, 120.
Establishment, the, 162 f.

Father (old man), 76 ff., 80.
Fear and Trembling, 21.
Frater Taciturnus, 124.

'Go farther', 98, 161.
God-relationship, 64 ff.
Governance (Providence), 64 ff., 91 f., 103, 138, 154.
Government, 162 f.

'High Priest', &c., 147.

Illusion, 22 ff., 30 ff., 40, 42, 47, 77, 90, 102, 140.
Immediacy, 73, 96.
Indirect communication, 25 ff., 148 f.
Individual, the, 20 f. 44, 61, 94, 102, 111 ff., 123 ff., 138, 152 f., 162 f.
Inter et Inter, 14, 150.
Irony, 54 f., 57 f.

Johannes Climacus, 150, 159.
Johannes de Silentio, 21.

INDEX

Laughter, a lover of, 125.
Legs, 101.
Leniency, 161.
Lilies of the Field, 147.
Lover, my, 62 f.

Maieutic, 148, 150.
Martyr, 90.
Melancholy, 76 ff.
Missionary, the, 138.
Misunderstanding, 123 ff., 138.
Møller, P. L., 95.

Numerical, 151.

Orthodox, the, 30.

Path of perdition, 80.
Pattern, the, 109.
Personal existence, 44 ff.
Philosophy, 146.
Poet (poetic), 68, 73, 84 f., 103, 133 f., 146, 159, 161.
Poet, my, 100 ff.
Polemical, 59.
Politician, 109.
Press, the, 44 f., 118 ff.
Protestations, 15 f.
Providence (Governance), 64 ff., 91 f., 103, 138, 154.

Pseudonyms, 13 f., 39 ff., 42, 85 f., 126, 146, 149, 161.
Public, the, 20 f., 59, 138, 151 f.

Race, 88 f., 89 f., 138.
Reduplication, 16 f., 151.
Reflection, 37 f., 42 f., 73, 89 f., 94, 96, 136, 148, 150.
Regina (a *factum*), 83 ff.
Religion (religious), 6, 25 ff., 30 f., 53 ff., 59 ff., 73 f., 147 ff., 155.
Religious awakening, 84.
Religious man, the, 109.

Satire, 165.
Sickness unto Death, 147.
Socrates, 6, 23, 41, 61, 138 f.
Spy, 87 f., 89, 95.
String, a new, 91.
'Superior', 91 f.
System, the, 42, 75, 97, 131.

Tactics, 38, 159 ff.
'take notice', 34 ff., 149.
Teleological suspension, 91.
Thorn in the flesh, 82.
Training in Christianity, 162.
Two Minor Treatises, 146.

Unconditional, the, 163 ff.

Victor Eremita, 18.

'Without authority', 75, 130, 147, 155, 159.
Witness for the truth, 46, 117, 132.
Works of Love, 134, 150.